MW01264293

FROM CRACKERS...
TO CAVIAR

FROM CRACKERS...
TO CAVIAR

A GUIDE TO PERSONAL DEVELOPMENT

JAMES R. COOPER

From Crackers to Cavier
By James R. Cooper

© Copyright 2010 by James R. Cooper
Maxser Publishing
P.O. Box 20147
Towson, Maryland 21284
www.fromcrackerstocaviar.com

Unless otherwise identified, Scripture quotations are taken from the HOLY BIBLE, NEW INTERNATIONAL VERSION Copyright 1973,1978, 1984 by the International Bible Society. Used by permission of Zonderevan Publishing House. All rights reserved.

Library of Congress Cataloging-in-Publication Data
Cooper, James Robert (James Robert Cooper), 1965-. From Crackers to Caviar A Guide to Personal Development/ James Robert Cooper.—1st ed p.cm.
Summary: A personal development guide which uses biblical principals as it teaches you to reach inwardly to achieve your success.
ISBN 978-0-984667-0-2
1. Christian Life – Personal Development – Motivation & Inspiration.

All rights reserved. No part of this publication may be reproduced or transmitted in any form or by any means, electronic or mechanical, including photocopying, recording, or by any information storage and retrieval system, without the prior written permission from the publisher or the author. Contact the publisher for information on foreign rights.

ISBN: 978-0-9844667-0-2

PRINTED IN THE UNITED STATES OF AMERICA

This book is dedicated to my
Father-in-Law, George Allen.
Mr. George, you are not here to read
this book, but many of the things
I have learned from you are in these words.
I miss you Pop Pop.

George Allen
May 24, 1947 – Nov 5, 2006

FOREWORD

"Is there yet another son," is what Samuel the Prophet said to Jesse the Bethlehemite. It was time to set another King in place for what was at hand for the future of the children of Israel. An anointing ceremony was about to take place, a time that would unveil the one God chose to lead a people. Some *protocols* were going to be broken and history will be made. The seven sons of Jesse passed before Samuel. Although one may have had the look of a leader, the Lord specifically spoke to Samuel to say not to look on the outward appearance but to look at the heart of the man. After the seven sons were not approved by God, Samuel asked Jesse, "Is there another son." Of course, the tradition was that the eldest son would surely be the first and wisest choice. Surely, Samuel knew that he heard the Lord. Where is the ONE God was speaking of? Samuel the Prophet of God was not about to leave without accomplishing this divine mandate of anointing the next leader. Of course you know the story of how Jesse describes the "one" son that he did not think to invite to the anointing ceremony (David) as the one who is the youngest and looks after the sheep. Surely, David did not fit the mold of the next reigning leader. History was confirmed and completed that day. The one who was the least likely to rule stepped into a place with God where all the rules were broken.

James Cooper is also a man whom God has broken protocols. He is a man of great humility who has no letters behind his name by man's standard but has the approval from heaven to mentor, train and lead His people. His stature is of a man 6'3. His educational background has not taken him to the places God has taken him. His lineage did not do it either. This guy has had the privilege of mentoring several high level dignitaries. He has counseled many business men and women with his motto being "success is non-negotiable." He is a great husband and father.

This book will walk you through some of his pitfalls and victories for life, and give you practical and humorous strategies for living your life to your fullest. To sit with James for just a short period of time will change your destiny forever.

I am very honored and proud to unveil to you one who God has broken "protocols" for. May the world receive James Cooper as "bread." May you eat of his pitfalls and victories and ask God to break protocols for you.

Dr. Cheryl Hill
D.Div

ACKNOWLEDGEMENTS

I give all honor and glory to my Savior, the Lord Jesus Christ. He alone has blessed me with this incredible message and I thank Him for all that He means to my life. I can do all things through Christ who strengthens me.

To my wife and partner Regyna and to our son Andrew. You have both blessed me beyond measure. You put up with me as I buried myself away to complete this work. I love you both dearly.

To my parents Bob and Anna Cooper.

> *"I will fight no more forever. It is not that I won't fight, it is that I won't fight with weapons or with violence any more. Instead, I will fight with the wisdom of*

my father and the compassion of my mother."
– Native American Chief Joseph

Mom and Dad, thank you. This is your success. I am the vessel it is being poured through to the world.

To my Mother-in-Law Mae Allen. Mom, you showed me what true love is. You have a priceless heart, and I cannot thank you enough for what you mean to me. I love you so much.

To family, near and far! Thank you for being you. This project would have never been born without you. Daniel, you won!

To Roland. It has been a long journey. Your friendship and counsel has made this possible. I am forever grateful to have you in my life.

To Dr. Cheryl. Keep building leaders. I appreciate all you have done and all you will do. I am honored to be a small part of what you do.

To Pastor Claudia. A thousand thanks. You continue to bless me. Keep pressing.

To my book coach Mia Redrick. You did it; you got water from a rock! I aspire to be the coach and mentor you are. A million thanks to you.

To Carolyn. Thank you for the graphics. You were given a vague idea and made it awesome.

To Circle of Champions. Bob, thank you for showing me my destiny. May God continue to bless the works of your hands. To all my friends from COC, Mack, Alisha, Sherry, there are too many to name. I'm looking forward to seeing what's next.

To Pastor Jeff and the team at Whitehorse. Thank you for showing me what 'sold out' really means.

To Dr. Jeff Magee. I thank God every day for the open seat next to you!

To Willie Jolley. Willie, thank you for walking off your job so many years ago. You opened the door for so many to discover their greatness. God's blessings upon you and Dee.

To all those who have a vision. Your time is now.

CONTENTS

Section Three – Excellence

Section Four – Determination

INTRODUCTION

By James Cooper

The S.E.E.D.s of success

> *Job 8:7* Your beginnings will seem humble, so prosperous will your future be.

I didn't start out planning to write a book. But God had a better plan.

That seems to be a strange way to start your own book, but it is the truth. I am a man who would read everything in front of me, books, magazines, cereal boxes, anything. But I never in a million years thought I would write a book. But then some things started to change.

I was working for a company in the Washington D.C. area. I was making great money, had a good title and great benefits, I had a great wife and an incredible son. But I was miserable. I knew I was supposed to be doing more. I had always wanted to help people with their problems, but I felt like I wasn't qualified. Every personal development book, every success guide I read seemed to be written by great men and women with a long list of letters behind their names. That wasn't me. So I thought I could start over once I finished working and do what I loved.

All that changed one hot Mid Atlantic afternoon. A co-worker and friend and I were standing on a sidewalk in Washington, D.C, when he asked me a question that changed the course of my life. "If you could do anything, and didn't have to worry about money, what would you do?" My response was immediate, "That's easy, I'd talk to people about how to achieve great things in their lives." He quietly told me, "You know, there's a whole industry that does that. Have you heard of Motivational Speakers?"

It's funny how and where God will touch you in a special way. Jesus called the Apostle Peter at a pier, Paul on the Damascus Road, Moses in a desert. As for me, my calling began on a sidewalk in Washington, D.C. That one conversation led to the writing of this book, and so much more in my life.

This book is an expanded work of a message I give when I speak in schools, colleges, businesses, and ministries. The Lord gave me the keynote message of the S.E.E.D.s of Success. Each letter of the word seed became an acronym for the success principle. We all have seeds of greatness inside of us. But because of the noise and pace of life, we forget about them, or tune them out entirely. This message teaches people to reach inwardly, and nourish these seeds by following a simple four step process.

1. **Sight:** See your Success clearly

2. **Execution:** Act on what you see inside you.

3. **Excellence:** Do your best in all things everyday, and watch your results

4. **Determination:** Let nothing stop you from seeing your vision become a reality.

The book is divided into four sections; each section is based on one of these principals. Each chapter stands as an individual lesson, so you can go to any section you feel drawn to and begin. You do not have to review each chapter in order to benefit from the book. It is designed to meet you, the reader, wherever you are stuck at that moment.

I delivered this message for years, and many times after I finished speaking, someone would ask me if I had a book. I always said I was going to write it, or I was too busy chasing my dreams to write it now. But the reality was I was still listening to an inner voice who kept telling me I wasn't qualified to write a personal development book. I was paralyzed by the same fear I had helped thousands overcome with the words given to me by the Lord.

One of my opening statements that I often start a message with is, "My success is non-negotiable!" I tell the audience, if you make success non-negotiable, your habits, wants and desires will change. Well, I finally did the same in relation to writing a book. I made it non-negotiable. Suddenly all of the obstacles that held me back disappeared. The help I needed to make this dream a reality came to me without me asking. My desires lined up with the will of God in my life, and a book was born.

As you read this book, keep in mind the words are tools to help you find your way to discovering what your assignment is, and who you are here to bless. Like any tool, they are of no use on the shelf. You have to learn how to master each one. Read a chapter over and over until it is planted deep in you, fertilizing the seed the Lord placed there before you were born. These plans have lain dormant for too long. As the Lord told young Jeremiah in Jeremiah 29:11, "For I know the plans I have for you," declares the LORD, "plans to prosper you and not to harm you, plans to give you hope and a future."

My prayer for you is that the Lord uses this book to help you make your success non-negotiable, to give you, and those who you are assigned to help, a great future.

James Cooper
Towson, Maryland

SECTION ONE
SIGHT

In this section we identify what we see, or visualize. If we are to become successful, we have to see our world in a different way. We will start on the success trail by pointing some of the concepts used to change the way we view our situation, opportunities, and challenges. How we can break free of long held ideas of what is true, and what is possible. As we change our thinking, we will start to see new results. Before we can look to our environment, we have to take a long look at our INvironment. Like Malcolm Forbes said, "the best vision is insight."

CHAPTER ONE
MIND-SIGHT

2 Kings, chapter 6 verses 15-17:

¹⁵ When the servant of the man of God got up and went out early the next morning, an army with horses and chariots had surrounded the city. "Oh, my lord, what shall we do?" the servant asked.

¹⁶ "Don't be afraid," the prophet answered. "Those who are with us are more than those who are with them."

¹⁷ And Elisha prayed, "O LORD, open his eyes so he may see." Then the LORD opened the servant's eyes, and he looked and saw the hills full of horses and chariots of fire all around Elisha.

I can relate with what the servant of Elisha experienced. Here was a man who was walking with a prophet, a man of God, who has seen incredible miracles during his time with Elisha. On this morning he wakes up and sees that generation's version of a tank division of the U.S. Army surrounding him. Just like waking up today and seeing an armed group surrounding your home, he immediately thought they were in serious trouble. But hold on a second, this servant was with Elisha when an ax fell in the water, and Elisha threw a stick where it fell, and the ax head floated. He was there when Elisha repeatedly told the King of Israel where the King of Aram was sending his troops to attack the Israelites. So this servant had seen some incredible miracles happen through Elisha. But on this morning he believed what he saw with his *natural eyes* and immediately accepted what he saw as fact and as truth. But the truth was much more than his eyes could see.

Many of us are blocked from our success because we accept what we see in everyday life. We often believe there are no other options, no other ways: all we have is what we see in front of us. What we currently *believe* we see is exactly what tells us there are no other ways to achieve the things we say we want. This see, think and believe approach is holding us back from achieving the results we say we desire.

There's an old saying that says, "seeing is believing," and I believe that's absolutely true. I believe many of us accept exactly what we choose to see. Another way to say it is, "what you see is what you get." Whatever you see, you believe and accept, therefore, what you see is exactly what you receive in life.

But is there more?

What about your inner sight, your imagination? What about your ability to visualize and see a different outcome? In Psalms 8:5-6, David tells us who we really are; the abilities God has given man:

> [5] *You made him (man) a little lower than the heavenly beings and crowned him with glory and honor.*

> [6] *You made him ruler over the works of your hands; you put everything under his feet.*

The works of God's hands and everything under our feet is this world! Now, how was this world created? God spoke what He saw and it was so. To a lesser extent, we have the same ability. The ability to create our world based on what we see, not with physical eyes, but with our inner eyes. Let me give you an example. Everything you see around you right now this very instant was once someone's idea. If you're inside an office, you see desks, chairs, printers, computers and copiers. If you're in a home, you see floors, carpets, furniture, appliances, art, and electronics surrounded by four walls. All these things, and even the buildings, were created by somebody. If you're walking in a park, someone designed the natural areas, the sidewalks, ponds, playgrounds; you get the idea.

A long time ago, this world was once all water, soil, rocks and plants; that's all man had to start with. From this, man turned this world into something created from his own mind. He took control and molded his world.

What are you creating within your mind? What mental boxes do you put yourself into everyday that you have created for yourself? What is your 'what you see is what you get'?

Mind-sight

Have you ever seen the 1999 movie *The Matrix*? There's a line in the movie in which the character Morpheus tries to explain this concept to the Chosen One, Neo.

> *"Have you ever had a dream Neo? A dream that you were so sure was real? What if you were unable to wake from that dream? How would you know the difference between the dream world, and the real world?"*

As a child, I had dreams that seemed so real, when they ended I wasn't sure if I was awake or asleep. I would awaken in a dark room believing I was still in the dream. Without my ability to see I wasn't sure whether I was awake or still dreaming; I couldn't define my reality. This is the power of mind-sight. Your mind is the most powerful natural tool you have. Mind-sight is using your mind to visualize and create the world you desire. Every man, woman, and child in this world sees their world based on what their mind sees first. Many of our great contemporaries have used their minds to create new and incredible businesses, works of arts, and scientific breakthroughs. Bill Gates created Microsoft on technology which was unheard of at the time. People had doubts about personal computers, yet he saw an opportunity, and made it his mission to put a personal computer on every person's desk and in every person's home. Now, back then, PCs weren't available at your local store for several hundred dollars. Personal computers cost thousands of dollars; they were big, and they used a lot of power, so the thought of people having one in their home was reserved for the very wealthy. But Gates kept moving forward. Although he fell short of his goal, no one will say Bill Gates was unsuccessful. He literally changed the world. Today, you can't say the word "Microsoft" anywhere in the world without someone recognizing the company and the man, and although it wasn't his initial goal, he also became one of the richest men in the world along the way.

What about our mind-sight? You don't have to want to start a software company, maybe you want to build something. Let's look at another example; the Empire State Building. The Empire State Building was built in 1930. At the time, it was the world's largest and tallest building at 102 stories. It was not just built to be the world's tallest building, no, the builders had a vision. They saw businessmen lining up to have their business address at 350 5th Ave, New York, NY. Now remember, the Empire State Building was built in the 1930s with 410 days worth of steel and sweat-that is 18 months to erect the tallest skyscraper in the world.

The major obstacle the builders encountered was a real doozy. The country was right in the midst of the Great Depression. The economy of the time was in a complete shambles. People were barely surviving; they were losing homes, unable to find work, and living in a depressed situation. Consequently, the building sat vacant most of the time due to its location. You see, at the time, there was no subway or mass transit access to the building, unlike their major competitor The Chrysler Building, located on a busy thoroughfare and accessible by public transit.

What the owners of the Empire State Building did to create the illusion of occupancy was sheer brilliance. During the evenings, the owners would send people from floor to floor turning on and off lights inside the empty offices. This gave the illusion to onlookers that people were in offices, working late, and using the building. Because of this, people started moving in and creating their own space. Transit access followed and growth took place.

What is absolutely amazing is that in 1931, this monstrosity of a building cost 40 million dollars to construct, and the building did not become profitable until 1950. That's 19 years of having this structure in the red every year. Finally, in 1951 the owners sold the building for a then record 51 million dollars.

Through all the adversity, they saw what it could be. They focused on nothing else. Because of their mind-sight, we now have a world famous landmark. Now it's a place for us to visit and enjoy for its grandeur and splendor. Like the owners imagined, the Empire State Building is one of the prime locations to have your business. No one else saw what those men eventually created. What they saw in their minds, we are blessed to see with our eyes.

I humbly submit to you that who you are right now, this very second, is a direct result of your thinking; your view of who you are, what you have, and your outlook on your situation. As a kid, when I was feeling down about myself, or whatever problem I was working through, my Dad would often say to me, "The man with no shoes feels sorry for himself until he sees the man with no feet." I knew then I'd better take a different look at my situation, my dad wasn't going to join me on the pity highway. If you are struggling, the thing holding you back may simply be the fact you're using your *physical eyes,* and they are trapping and preventing your *spiritual eyes*-your visionary eyes-from seeing the possibilities.

Call to Action: Clean Lines of Sight

First, you must identify who you are. We recognize ourselves by our names, we recognize ourselves by our jobs, we even recognize ourselves by our positions in our families and by material status.

Is this really who we are?

Who we are is the sum of our experience, our beliefs, and what we are designed to do with our lives. In Jeremiah 1:5, the Lord spoke to the teen Jeremiah and told him,

> [5] *"Before I formed you in the womb I knew you, before you were born I set you apart; I appointed you as a prophet to the nations."*

So who are we?

Here's an exercise a mentor did for me many years ago. I adopted it and added it to my coaching program.

The 25 Word Test

This exercise works best with someone to hold you accountable. You have to identify who you are in 25 words or less, in sentence form. You can't identify yourself by your name. You can't identify yourself by your family status; you can't say mom, dad, brother or sister, father of, or son of, or uncle of; and you cannot define your identity by your vocation. You cannot describe your identity by who your friends say you are. You have to dig down deep and, using only adjectives, describe who you are. *Your identity.*

You have one minute to complete this exercise.

_____

_____

_____

_____

_____

_____

_____

Steven Covey in his best selling book *7 Habits of Highly Effective People* says, in habit number two, to begin with the end in mind. Yes, your success must begin with the end in mind. This journey starts by knowing where you want to go. We may ultimately end up on a different path-and that's okay, but if you can't see where you want to go, you will never get there. This is why we must create a clear vision for ourselves in terms of where we are going to go and what we are going to do.

Call to Action: See Your Future

Go to a serene place. Take a few moments and relax. Go to your special place and get in prayer, meditation, a quiet state of mind. It's time to discover your future. Who are you five years from now? Where are you living? What are you driving? Who is around you? Are you single or married? Do you have children and if so, what is happening in their lives? Do you live in a house, rent an apartment, cruise the world in a yacht? Are you travelling? Are you in a motor home or jet setting around the world? What is your vocation? What is it that you do in this world? Who are you working for? Are you working for yourself? The clearer and more defined you make this vision, the better your opportunity for success.

Write out the vision you see. Don't stop writing until you have captured every detail. When you get back, take this vision and post it next to a place in your home where you will see it everyday. Put it in your bathroom; on your bedroom door, somewhere you can't help but see it. This is a living document. Let's say you want to be a dentist, and you start doing research. Three months later you realize you want to be an oral surgeon, spending 25% of your time doing work with orphaned children: write it down. Once you start this process, the person God has destined you to be will become clearer. Have fun!

_____

_____

_____

_____

_____

_____

_____

_____

CHAPTER TWO
BREAKING ALL THE RULES

Lord of the Sabbath, Mark, chapter 2 verses 23-27:

> ²³ *One Sabbath, Jesus was going through the grain-fields, and as his disciples walked along, they began to pick some heads of grain.*

> ²⁴ *The Pharisees said to him, "Look, why are they doing what is unlawful on the Sabbath?"*

> ²⁵ *He answered, "Have you never read what David did when he and his companions were hungry and in need?"*

²⁶ In the days of Abiathar the high priest, he entered the house of God and ate the consecrated bread, which is lawful only for priests to eat. And he also gave some to his companions."

²⁷ Then he said to them, "The Sabbath was made for man, not man for the Sabbath.

²⁸ So the Son of Man is Lord even of the Sabbath."

Here, Jesus was questioning the people of the ruling class of the time – challenging them on their beliefs – questioning whether what they believed was the truth. Let's be clear, Jesus never broke any of God's commandments or laws, but he did challenge the mindset and the beliefs of those ruling at the time, those who were oppressing the people.

Jesus' actions were quite challenging and revolutionary in a time when little tolerance was given to lawbreakers. I find it interesting that man makes rules or laws so complex most people simply can't understand them. You begin to wonder why these rules are put in place to begin with. Today, Christians walk under the Grace of the Salvation of Christ, but during Jesus' time, if you violated the Sabbath, stoning may have been your fate.

In order to achieve success, you must first be willing to break some rules that have been created within your mind over the years. These rules have come from many different places; from well meaning loved ones and from people we respect. We may have learned from our parents who taught us as they were taught, and we accepted their teachings as law. But these life rules can be adjusted. Look at new-lyweds. You have two people coming from different life experiences becoming one in marriage. I wonder how many times during those early years they rationalize their marriage beliefs with the phrase, "well, this is how I was raised" or, "this is how I was taught," and the last resort argument of, "that's all there is to it." Is there a deeper truth to this? Is there another way to come up with a better compromise that benefits everyone involved? What you've experienced and what you've seen has been built upon the compromised values of two other people. Yet, we accept it as faith – as gospel – as the way it's supposed to be and, "that's all there is to it." King David tells us in Psalms:

Psalms 119:59

> *I have considered my ways and have turned my*
> *steps to Your statutes.*

We have to challenge our thinking in order to achieve what we were designed to do over the course of our lives. We have to question the authority of self limiting beliefs, to break these values down and tear them apart. Many times, our own self imposed rules actually prevent us from having what we're supposed to receive in this life.

I love this quote from Gen. Douglas McArthur:

> *"Rules are mostly made to be broken and are too*
> *often for the lazy to hide behind."*

He didn't say that *all* rules are meant to be broken, and I'm not saying that you should ignore the law or just say anything you want, no matter what. In order for you to go to another level, and achieve things you never thought possible, you're going to have to do some different things. You're going to have to question the beliefs and ideology you have allowed yourself to operate within. You must construct new programming; generate new laws to operate from within your mind.

In the movie *The Matrix*, Morpheus made it his point to challenge Neo in every single aspect of his belief system. At one point Morpheus challenges Neo, asking if he feels a bit like Alice tumbling down the rabbit hole. Neo agrees and Morpheus tells him that his eyes show it, saying, "You have the look of a man who accepts what he sees because you are expecting to wake up." Ironically, that's not far from the truth. Neo says that he doesn't believe in fate, and when asked why not, Neo replies, "I don't like the idea that I'm not in control over my own life."

Neo's answer is ironic. The challenge is that we want to be in total control – too much in control of our lives. We have boxed ourselves in. We take what we see and accept it as fact. Anytime we do that, we stop thinking. *We actually stop the creative process.*

In Chapter One, I referred to the team who built the Empire State Building. The Empire State building was actually modeled from a much smaller building already in existence. That building was built at the turn of the previous century in Winston Salem, North Carolina. That building was only 130 feet tall – barely one-tenth the size of the Empire State Building. It was used as a template, a predecessor; it provided tangible beginnings of something that could be built on a much larger scale.

What could we accomplish if we thought on a larger scale? If we could just break the rules in our minds? Remember Bill Gates? His goal was unprecedented at the time because no one understood the value of the personal computer. When they first came out, they cost $3000, yet Bill Gates believed computers would be a staple in every home and business in the world.

A great example of a rule breaker is Samuel Truett Cathy. Truett Cathy is the CEO of the fast food chain Chick-Fil-A. The chain was born in the state of Georgia in the year 1946, and it now consists of over 1300 restaurants in 37 states. What sets this chain apart from other fast food chains is the fact that all their restaurants are closed on Sundays. This is highly unusual as Sundays are typically a high sales day for this type of business. To close on Sunday means the owners give up huge amounts of profit every week-and restaurants operate on very slim profit margins.

This is breaking a traditional rule in the restaurant business, yet Cathy decided to do it when he first opened his doors. He did something else unique too; he opened his stores in shopping centers. This broke with the logic of the time because almost all restaurants were in stand-alone buildings. He saw a way to recoup some of his losses from being closed on Sundays by not having to incur the expense of building stand-alone stores. So, did breaking from the norm work for Chick-Fil-A? As of 2008, the Chick-Fil-A Franchise has had 40 straight years of business growth. Cathy explained closing on Sundays by saying:

> *"I was not so committed to financial success that I was willing to abandon my principles and priori-*

ties. One of the most visible examples of this is our decision to close on Sunday. This decision was our way of honoring God, and to directing our attention to things that matter more than our business."

Here's a businessman who is saying there are more important things in life than business. That type of thinking is outside the norm. This is similar to what Jesus was trying to teach the Pharisees in his example. Not everything is written in stone. We've heard that said before. Not everything *is* as you believe it has to be. Perhaps there's a deeper truth that you must explore.

In order to achieve what you have been destined for, you must locate a deeper level of truth: you must find a new way. If not, you will simply be following someone else's version of the truth and you will find yourself empty and unfulfilled.

People once thought it was impossible to escape the gravitational pull of the earth. Now, after countless rocket launches, we have a different understanding. The four minute mile was impossible until Sir Roger Bannister proved everyone wrong. Immediately after Bannister's historic run, with the barrier now broken, men started consistently running sub four minute miles. Be contrary in your thinking. Remember, thoughts become things and in order to achieve what you have never thought possible, you need to challenge your thinking. Keep in mind that what's considered to be the norm today was once cutting edge. Cars once had carburetors, bias-ply tires, drum brakes and AM radios. Now they have fuel injection, radial tires, disc brakes and premium sound navigation centers. Remember the old, standard rotary phone? Now many people have cordless home phones and a cell phone. At one time, even owning a phone was a luxury. Fifty years ago, owning a television was a luxury. Now multiple Hi-Def televisions in the home are common.

If you want to change your success – change what you believe is possible. Upgrade your belief system, trade your old system in for a newer model. Change what you believe reality and truth are – *your personal reality and your personal truth* – then start breaking down the old rules!

Keep in mind that for each rule you challenge, people will look at you in a different light, because you now see things from a different perspective. Take cigarette smoking. Smokers are an interesting bunch of folks. As long as you're a smoker, you're part of the clique – you against all the non-smokers. Many smokers who stop smoking come to view the habit as disgusting and can't believe they smoked at all. That's because they now know a deeper truth. Ex-smokers have told me they can taste food better, breathe better, and even smell better. Many former smokers become anti-smoking zealots in an effort to try and stop the whole world from smoking because of their own life changing experience when they discovered a deeper truth. Discover the deeper truth about you and the success you were designed for. Break free of your self imposed rules.

Call to Action: Breaking Down Old Beliefs

Write down three things you want to change to achieve your new beliefs. They may be related to business, family, money, or relationships. Challenge each belief you list, and write down why you believe in them and why you support that belief. This takes a certain level of emotional maturity. Remember, these beliefs were passed down to us by our mentors, our parents, and from people who were influential in our lives, or by habit. By challenging these actions or beliefs, you're not saying they are wrong, you are recognizing there is a deeper level of truth that you must discover about yourself in order to grow.

Use your five-year vision as a base. On one side of a sheet of paper, write down your current beliefs. On the other side, write your challenge to that belief. It should look something like the example below:

My Belief	My Challenge To That Belief
iPods are the only type of portable music player you can buy. I believe this because it's the only handheld device I see on T.V. commercials	In reality, you can buy an iPOD, MS Zune, Scandisk, Sony or other types of MP3 players.

<table>
<tr><td></td><td></td></tr>
<tr><td></td><td></td></tr>
</table>

Once you have accepted the new level of truth, pick the next three to address. I do this exercise each time I know change is about to occur in my life. Don't become discouraged if you find yourself slipping back to your old beliefs. You are addressing a lifetime of program-ming. It will take your subconscious time to accept the new rules. But, once you have, you will see immediate progress!

CHAPTER THREE
MINDSET MATTERS

Numbers, chapter 13 verses 26-33:

> *²⁶ They came back to Moses and Aaron and the whole Israelite community at Kadesh in the Desert of Paran. There they reported to them and to the whole assembly and showed them the fruit of the land.*

> *²⁷ They gave Moses this account: "We went into the land to which you sent us, and it does flow with milk and honey! Here is its fruit.*

> *²⁸ But the people who live there are powerful and the*

cities are fortified and very large. We even saw descendants of Anak there.

29 The Amalekites live in the Negev; the Hittites, Jebusites and Amorites live in the hill country; and the Canaanites live near the sea and along the Jordan."

30 Then Caleb silenced the people before Moses and said, "We should go up and take possession of the land, for we can certainly do it."

31 But the men who had gone up with him said, "We can't attack those people; they are stronger than we are."

32 And they spread among the Israelites a bad report about the land they had explored. They said, "The land we explored devours those living in it. All the people we saw there are of great size.

33 We saw the Nephilim there (the descendants of Anak come from the Nephilim). We seemed like grasshoppers in our own eyes, and we looked the same to them."

To give you some background information, in this chapter Moses sent twelve men into the Promised Land after the Israelites had left Egypt, and had them scout the land. They went into the land and saw that what had been prophesied or spoken of by God was indeed correct. The land was full of fruit and honey; full of all the people needed.

Although they saw the good, they also saw problems. They saw huge men, the descendents of giants. These men were tall and powerfully built. They were trained in the ways of war from their youth. Now, you have to remember the children of Israel at the time were people who had been slaves, so they were not warriors, they were not people who had been taught to wage war. They were builders; architects; they were people who had built the great pyramids and other wondrous structures in Egypt. Not exactly the skills necessary for taking land occupied by warriors.

Two of the men who went into the land, Joshua and Caleb, said, "We should take this land. Let's go get it, we are able!" The other ten men said, "No, there are giants in that land. If we go in there, we will die."

Later, we are told two men gave a good report and ten other men gave an evil report. All twelve men saw the same thing, but how their minds perceived what they saw made the difference. Two men saw the opportunity; ten men saw defeat. The two men were right. You see, it is all about your mindset, and the type of information you allow your mind to see.

In Chapter One we spoke of mind-sight, how you see things with your mind and how you manifest or materialize those things before they are created. Mind-sight is incredibly important. But your mind-sight can only see what your mindset allows. Your mindset is the foundation for all of the things you know to be fact; the things you believe to be true, regardless of whether they are or are not.

For instance, at one point in history people believed the world to be flat, until it was proven otherwise by the discovery that the world was round, or indeed a ball shape. The same thing happens to us every single day of our lives, and it is what we choose to believe that either limits us or allows us to succeed in life.

The person who created the term "mindset" was a mentor of mine sometime back, a man named Bill Bailey, and the first time he and I spoke he adjusted my mindset. I told him I had a burning desire to be an inspirational speaker and to deliver my message of living life to the fullest, maximizing your potential, and doing everything possible to achieve the greatness bestowed upon us all. He encouraged me: he told me that I would be a great speaker one day, and I told him that it would take me years to learn to achieve this lofty goal. He immediately adjusted my mindset.

Now in his 70s, he is a much older gentleman than me. He has been the coach of Les Brown, the late Jim Rohn, and many other tremendous speakers. He had a multi-level marketing business in the 1970s making 64 million dollars a month across 11 countries, selling soap! So he knows a little bit about success. What he told me that day was this:

> *"Young man, man created the twenty-four hour clock. He could have easily created an eighteen hour clock or a thirty-six hour clock. Time is a series of emotional experiences and the intensity of those emotions."*

What he did for me with those words was help me to realize that if I wanted to be a great speaker, and if I wanted to do it quickly, I had to put more experiences under my belt in a shorter amount of time. In three sentences, Bill Bailey adjusted my mindset.

It did not require five or ten years, or whatever number was in my mind, to achieve my goal; it required the opportunity to get out there and do it, and do it often enough to gain valuable experiences. This is the essence of adjusting your mindset. Remember, it took a few sentences to give me a new understanding of the truth. Hall of Fame motivational speaker Willie Jolley wrote a book titled, *It Only Takes a Minute to Change Your Life.* Truer words have never been written. In less than one minute, my life changed.

We said in Chapter Two, in order to achieve what you believe you want, in order to be successful, you have to challenge self-limiting beliefs. There is a clear path of distinction between the thinking of successful and unsuccessful people. One distinctive trait of unsuccessful people is a tendency to keep looking back. They look back at what they have done, or what other people have done, and they call that "fact" – when it is not necessarily true.

Sir Roger Bannister was the first person to run a sub four-minute mile. Until he did, no-one believed it was possible, but what I find most interesting is that almost immediately after his achievement, several other people also achieved it – instantly breaking Bannister's record. What this demonstrates is a change of mindset; people were now willing to challenge common belief.

> *"Doctors and scientists said that breaking the four-minute mile was impossible, that one would die in the attempt. Thus, when I got up from the track after*

collapsing at the finish-line, I figured I was dead."
– *Roger Bannister*

During my time and in my studies, I've seen a clear difference between people who have successful mindsets and unsuccessful mindsets. The Unsuccessful look back. They live in their past, exist in their present, and fear their future. The Successful *remember* their past, *live* in their present, and *plan* their future.

Unsuccessful people hold on to their past, remembering only what has already happened and allowing the events of the past to influence everything about their present and future. For example, if a person tried to start a business, but failed, they may never try again. Successful people remember past experiences but they're able to use the past events as lessons for their future pursuits. "Okay, this business didn't work, but I have a better understanding of what it will take to make the next one work. Let's move forward." I love this great quote from the powerful motivational speaker Les Brown:

> *"If I fall down, I want to fall on my back because if I*
> *can look up, then I can get up."*

The difference between a successful and an unsuccessful mindset is simply perception. You have to recognize, and decide how you filter information in your mind. The same information can be perceived entirely differently, depending on your mindset.

The great author James Allen wrote a timeless masterpiece now considered to be the grandfather of all self-help books, *As A Man Thinketh*. The title comes from the Bible, Proverbs 23:7, "For as he thinketh in his heart, so is he." Allen's wise words have inspired generations, as have the wise words found in the book of Proverbs, written mainly by the wisest man to ever walk the earth, King Solomon, son of King David. Both great kings understood the power of thoughts and mindset. So should we.

Two people see the same situation; it is how they interpret it within the filters of their minds that make all the difference. The mindset they have dictates whether they see an opportunity or an obstacle. Every decision *you* make is another step towards your future. So how important is it to ensure you are doing everything you can to take the right steps?

In Philippians 4: 8-9, it says:

> [8] *Finally, brothers, whatever is true, whatever is noble, whatever is right, whatever is pure, whatever is lovely, whatever is admirable—if anything is excellent or praiseworthy—think about such things.*

> [9] *Whatever you have learned or received or heard from me, or seen in me—put it into practice. And the God of peace will be with you.*

What was Paul telling the Philippians? He was telling them, if you look at circumstances in a positive light, if you look for the good in every situation, if you look for the best in everyone, and if you follow my instructions as I have taught you, then God will be with you and everything will be just fine, everything will work according to His plan for your life.

You must consider your situation and look at it with a different set of eyes-your mind's eyes, referred to in Chapter Two. Look at the well known international author Robert Kiyosaki. In his book, *Rich Dad Poor Dad,* he tells a story of two different lives. The story is really about two different mindsets; a parable of the mindset of a rich dad and the mindset of a poor dad. It is one of my favorite audio books and I listen to it often. If you study it long enough, you get a clear picture of the two mindsets he was exposed to at an early age, and how both mindsets have played important roles in his life. At the end of the day, he realized what it was from each mindset he wanted to attach himself to.

Robert Kiyosaki understood the importance of formal education, but he also understood the importance of financial education, and he attached himself to the mindset of an entrepreneur, as opposed to the mindset of an employee. He believed in making his money work for him and adopted a self sufficient, rather than a dependent, attitude. He learned to look for opportunities, rather than being satisfied with a job and salary. He believed in getting out there and finding his own success as opposed to being content working for someone else, effectively letting them dictate his level of success.

> *"Remember your mind is your greatest asset, so be careful what you put into it."*
> – Robert Kiyosaki

Changing your outlook on life is a journey. Before beginning, you must prepare for your journey. This means taking a look at your current mindset. Is your current mindset holding you back? To change your success, and the overall outcome of your life, you must be prepared to change the rules you currently play by; you must address how you think and how you receive, reflect, and react in all situations. What's needed is a mind reset. My good friend Mary Elizabeth Murphy writes about this in her book, *Reset Your Buttons.* She teaches how to have more productive relationships in business and personally by resetting how you react towards negativity. Over the years, Mary Elizabeth has helped me realize that by creating a different mindset for dealing with obstacles, you can create a different outcome.

Call to Action: Mind Reset

Your language is a key indicator to your thinking. You may have heard the old expression, "watch what you say." This is exactly what we will do.

Over the next 30 days, track what you say regarding the things you want to achieve. You may want to carry positive statements with you to help you through the transition. Keep score of your language, one point taken away for a negative statement, and two points added for a positive statement. When you catch yourself saying a negative statement but then change yourself immediately, you get one point. So by catching yourself saying a negative statement, and correcting yourself, you still win!

Do not become discouraged, you are changing a lifetime of beliefs. Keep a journal to track your progress. Find an accountability part-ner; someone to walk through the changes with you. This exercise will help you to break down the limits of your mind. Martial arts expert Bruce Lee once said:

> *"If you always put limits on everything you do, physical or anything else, it will spread into your work and into your life, there are no limits, there are only plateaus and you must not stay there, you must go beyond them."*

SECTION TWO
EXECUTION

In this section we explore the barriers that stop you from moving forward on the road to being a success. Seeing your vision is a great start, but if you never do anything to see your dreams come true, you will have lived an incomplete life. We will explore the things that may stop you from getting started. Fear, self limiting beliefs, procrastination, and working through change are challenges that must be addressed each time we move to a new level. No matter how much you accomplish, you must overcome these roadblocks.

CHAPTER FOUR
FEARSTORMS

Matthew, chapter 14 verses 25-33:

> *25 During the fourth watch of the night Jesus went out to them, walking on the lake.*

> *26 When the disciples saw him walking on the lake, they were terrified. "It's a ghost," they said, and cried out in fear.*

> *27 But Jesus immediately said to them, "Take courage! It is I. Don't be afraid."*

²⁸ "Lord, if it's you," Peter replied, "tell me to come to you on the water."

²⁹ "Come," he said. Then Peter got down out of the boat, walked on the water and came toward Jesus.

³⁰ But when he saw the wind, he was afraid and, beginning to sink, cried out, "Lord, save me!"

³¹ Immediately Jesus reached out his hand and caught him. "You of little faith," he said, "why did you doubt?"

³² And when they climbed into the boat, the wind died down.

³³ Then those who were in the boat worshipped him, saying, "Truly you are the son of God."

Peter, for a brief moment walked outside of his fear. As an experienced fisherman, he understood the power of the sea, and had a healthy respect for it. If fishing then was like fishing is today, some of his friends never returned from fishing trips, and he feared drowning. But yet for a moment, with the urging of Jesus, he stepped out of his fear and into his faith. As Jesus points out, faith will always triumph over fear. As you adopt these new strategies, you will have to learn how to manage your fear. If you do not manage your fear, it can take on a life of its own, and grow until you are stuck in the middle of a fearstorm

A fearstorm is when fear gets out of control and becomes a destructive force. You could say they're just like the thunderstorms experienced most afternoons on the east coast during the summer. The conditions build up with heat and humidity in the air but instead of resulting in a rainstorm, or even a torrential rainstorm, the end result is a thunderstorm. Sometimes, when the conditions are just right, you can have intense storms called microbursts. The same thing happens in our minds. We walk around with fears every day. But many times we overcome these fears by simply gaining a new level of understanding of the situation we fear. Then along come those times when certain conditions build up; certain conditions that are just right for increasing our fear, and that fear gets out of control and takes over. We become paralyzed; we can't move forward; we can't achieve what we were destined to do; we can't succeed in life.

Fearstorms. What are they? How do we conquer them? How do we recognize that we're in the midst of a fearstorm? And most importantly, how do we get out of a fearstorm?

The conditions of your fearstorms are personal to you. You may have been hurt in your past. Perhaps you publicly failed and have to face the same scenario again. You may have been mercilessly taunted as a youth about your clothes, the way you talk, look, eat, smile. Whatever the situation, you take those things on board and they become the base. Once you have the base, you begin to add new conditions to it. Take for example, a bad economy. Perhaps a man named Sam grew up without many financial means. Sam believes the lack of money to be the cause of many painful memories. The fear of being without again is the base. Now it's 30 years later, and the economy is in bad shape. Sam is concerned, but able to manage through his fears. Then Sam gets laid off from his job. Now you have the makings of a fearstorm. The conditions are just right.

The base conditions may already have caused you to place certain limitations on your life. Then, all it takes is an unfortunate situation to occur, and you become even more paralyzed; even more frozen, and even more stuck by your situation. Now it feels like everything is starting to spiral out of control and the next thing you know, you're so completely paralyzed you can't think straight. You believe to try anything means certain doom. That's a fearstorm.

Fearstorms are grounded in the past and they are fuelled by the uncertainty of the future. You're afraid of what *may* happen based on negative past experiences. So how do you conquer a fearstorm? First, you have to accept that you have fears, and if your fears are not addressed, they will take over. One of the most powerful kings in the Bible, and certainly one of God's fiercest warriors, King David, recognized his own fears and wrote openly about them.

In Psalms 55:4-8, he says:

> *⁴ My heart is in anguish within me; the terrors of death assail me.*

> *⁵ Fear and trembling have beset me; horror has overwhelmed me.*

> *⁶ I said, "Oh, that I had the wings of a dove! I would fly away and be at rest –*

> [7] *I would flee far away and stay in the desert; Selah*
>
> [8] *I would hurry to my place of shelter, far from the tempest and storm."*

It says in the Bible, King David killed 10 thousand men with his own hands. He's a fierce warrior, yet he says his heart's in anguish. Terror and death are all around him and it constantly attacks him. The horror is overwhelming yet he pressed on. Later, we learn he realized his strength comes from the Lord who is within him, so he taps into his source, and remembers the things he's done well in his past. He is saying, "You know what, I can overcome this, and I will." We all have the ability to do the same.

We can all experience overwhelming fear in life, especially when we're trying to do something new. We must deal with these fears, just as King David did, by recognizing that we have fears. If we don't address these fears – fears of success, fears of failure, fears of embarrassment, fears of ridicule, fears that we aren't good enough to achieve – then we will stay an unwilling captive all our lives. In my own example, a big fear of mine was writing a book. I had a fear that I was not good enough, I didn't have the education, I didn't have the words to convey to people my message of change, to encourage people to live their lives with purpose. I had to address those fears to be able to move forward, so that I could be where I am right now.

What fears do you have that are holding you back from achieving greatness in your life?

"You must do the thing you cannot do ... You gain strength, courage, and confidence by every experience by which you really stop to look fear in the face. You are able to say to yourself, 'I lived through this horror. I can take the next thing that comes along."

– Eleanor Roosevelt

You must address your fears. Write out all of the fears you have in your life. Address them on a piece of paper, say what they are, read them out loud, and, if you have a very good friend, tell them what your fear is. Telling a friend can be very empowering. It's not that your friend should be expected to address your fear in any way, or even say anything about them, it's simply speaking openly about your fear which gives you power to overcome. Remember this, fear lives in the darkness of our minds and dies in the light of the truth, so if you expose your fear for what it is, you can overcome it.

Call to Action: Best and Worse Case Scenario

Write out your best and worse case scenario for whatever it is that's holding you back.

Best case scenario: Ask yourself, what's the best thing that could happen if I do this?

For me, in this case, I asked myself, what's the best thing that happens if I write this book? The answer that came to me was, if I can change one life with this book then it was worth the effort, it was worth overcoming the fear.

Worse case scenario: Ask yourself, what's the worse thing that can happen if I don't do this?

In my case, I answered, if I don't write this book I'll stay exactly where I am, stuck here with this book inside of me, keeping it all to myself, where it was never meant to live. Failing to reach even one person who may need to be encouraged with these words.

This is an exercise I do quite often. I write out a pros and cons sheet whenever I'm trying to work through the fear of taking on a new challenge. Write out your own best and worst case scenarios and try to work through each one as it relates to your own situation.

Call to Action: Find Inspiration

Another way to move forward is to find inspiration in others. Identify other people who've already achieved success in whatever it is you're trying to do. When I was in basic training in the Air Force many years ago, I'd encourage myself by remembering that there were one million people in the Air Force. If they had all made it, so could I! Everyone who had already achieved success in the Air Force was a source of inspiration at times when I thought I wouldn't make it. I used that inspiration to give me the strength to keep trying.

Remember, the Bible tells us there's nothing new under the sun, so someone is *doing* what you've tried to do. Find out who it is; use them as an example and let them inspire you to move forward.

Anne Frank once said:

> *"The best remedy for those who are afraid, lonely, or unhappy, is to go outside, somewhere they can be quiet, alone with the heavens, nature and God.*
>
> *Because only then does one feel that all is as it should be. God wishes to see people happy and to witness the simple beauty of nature."*

CHAPTER FIVE
WHAT DO YOU BELIEVE?

Mark, chapter 9 verse 23:

> [23] *"What do you mean, if I can?" Jesus asked, "Anything is possible if a person believes."*

I love this verse because it makes such a simple, yet clear, statement: If you can believe it, you can achieve it. It's a simple success principle, but it's one that many of us do not fully grasp.

If you are struggling in a particular area of your life, it may be because you don't think you can achieve it or that you don't think you deserve it. This is a self-limiting belief that must be attacked to overcome, and to become what we're designed to achieve.

Let's look at Muhammad Ali. Everybody knows Muhammad Ali for the many great things he's accomplished in his life. He has been lauded all over the world as a champion of peace as well as a champion in the boxing ring. But it's his early times I love most, the beginning of his professional career. As an amateur, he'd been World Champion and won Olympic gold as a light-heavyweight boxer. At the start of his professional career, he continued to create quite a bit of success for himself. In fact, he was undefeated with 19 wins and 15 knockouts when he went up against Sonny Liston for the heavyweight championship. Sonny Liston was considered by the sports world to be a man who could, and would, easily destroy Muhammad Ali. Now, we all know Muhammad Ali never shied away from making bold statements about himself, but there must have been a little bit of doubt in his mind because he won that fight – and he won it convincingly – but afterwards he said this:

> *"I don't have a mark on my face and I upset Sonny Liston, and I just turned twenty-two years old. I **must** be the greatest"*
> *– Muhammad Ali, 1965*

Muhammad Ali became just about as famous for his positive self-talk statements, including, "I *am* the greatest," as he did for his boxing ability. However, later in life he said, "I called myself the greatest long before I believed it." In so doing, he gave us a key to understanding the power of our words, what we say to ourselves and who we think we are.

> *"I **am** the greatest. I said that even before I knew I was"*
> *– Muhammad Ali*

Even though there were some doubts in his mind as he went through his trials and tribulations, and his ups and downs, Muhammad Ali still called himself the greatest until he believed it and started carrying himself that way. So who do you call yourself; what program is running in your mind? What are you saying about yourself every single day, every minute of every day? What is it that's driving you? Would you let someone say to you the words you say to yourself everyday?

There's a chapter in Jeremiah I love because it says so much about the power of your words. Jeremiah had been called by the Lord to be a prophet and voice to the nation of Israel. At this time we believe Jeremiah was a teenager. Chapter 1, verse 6 tells us what he said and verse 7 gives us the Lord's reply.

> [6] *"Ah, sovereign Lord," I said, "I do not know how to speak; I am only a child."*

> [7] *But the Lord said to me, "Do not say, 'I am only a child.' You must go to everyone I send you to and say whatever I command you to."*

Jeremiah had doubts, and he spoke out about them. He didn't believe he was worthy of this call on his life. "I'm not worthy," he said, but the Lord immediately corrected him and said, "No, no, no! Do not say that you're not worthy." This is because the Lord knew the power of words. After all, God *spoke* this universe into existence. If you say it, you'll believe it, then you'll see it. A great quote I read some years ago says it all.

"Whether you think you can or you can't, you're right"
– Henry Ford

Whether you say you can or you can't, you're right. You're absolutely right. You have to decide what you're going to believe and you have to decide how you're going to carry yourself: you have to make the decision that you *are* going to believe you *can* achieve great things.

In order to become a success, you must change your self-talk and you must believe what you speak out. I like looking at the example of Michael Jordan. Michael Jordan is in the basketball Hall of Fame, his name is known around the world, and, even though he retired from sport in 2003, he's still one of the most recognizable sports figures in the world today. Most people know that Michael Jordan was cut from the basketball team when he was a sophomore in high school but something not everyone realizes is that he *had* made the team the previous year. As a freshman he was on the team, he just wasn't very good, so when he got cut from the team, something was triggered in him. He had to decide who he was and he had to decide whether he was able to play basketball at the level that was required or not. He has since said this:

"I think that not making the varsity team really drove me to work at my game, and also taught me that if you set goals and work hard to achieve them, the hard work can pay off"
– Michael Jordan

So he believed immediately that he could do it. He set new goals for himself, to make the varsity team, and as they say, the rest is history.

So how do you set your goals? A key I use in my life and many, many successful people also use, are affirmations. Affirmations are positive statements that you make to yourself about what you want to go accomplish. Statements about who you are and what you're destined to be.

How do you use affirmations? The key here is that you must write them down; not type them, not get them out of a book, not get them online, but physically write them down. It has been said there is a direct link between writing something down and what you write becoming wired into your subconscious mind. So you write down your affirmations; write down the key statements about yourself and your life.

In my situation, when I first started speaking, I wrote the affirmation that I was a world class international speaker. At the time of writing it down, I had very little public speaking experience, having never spoken in front of more than 15 people, but that didn't matter. By writing that affirmation down; by looking at it, by saying it, and by saying it repeatedly over and over again, my subconscious accepted it and believed it. I also wrote the affirmation that I was an author, a world famous author. I wrote that particular affirmation 6 years before I started writing this book. It took 6 years for *me* to get there but it's not going to take *you* that long because you already understand the process!

Call to Action: Creating your Affirmations

Referring to the lists you created in the earlier mind-sight and mind-set exercises, make a new list of the top 5 areas you want to change to become the success you visualize for yourself. Begin to speak the changes you are achieving by writing them down as affirmations. For example, I wrote down, 'I am a world class speaker,' and by doing so, I began the process of speaking it into reality. Confirm your belief by repeating each affirmation every morning and every evening. Say each one out loud in a clear powerful voice, full of confidence, preferably in front of a mirror. Carry your affirmations with you as positive reinforcement everywhere you go; use them to reinforce the new behaviors of who you've become.

In Habakkuk 2:2 it says:

> [2] *Then the Lord replied, " Write down the revelation and make it plain on tablets so that a herald may run with it."*

We're told to write down our vision and to make it plain. Doing this will change your belief system and if you change your belief system, it will change the success that you are achieving in your life.

CHAPTER SIX
DO IT NOW

Ecclesiastes, chapter 9 verse 10:

> [10] *Whatever your hands find to do, do it with all your might, for in the grave, where you are going, there is neither working nor planning nor knowledge nor wisdom.*

What I love about this verse is that it talks about doing it now. Procrastination is one of the biggest challenges to finding your success.

> *"Procrastination is opportunity's assassin"*
> *– Victor Kiam*

A friend of mine, who is a speaker, likes to say that the biggest nation in the world is procrastination, because so many people seem to live there. Overcoming procrastination is key to achieving any of the success you have set out before yourself.

The first question must be; why do people procrastinate to begin with; why do they stop themselves from achieving the success they believe they so richly deserve? Here are some of the reasons I have used, and some of the most common I have heard during my coaching sessions:

- **fear of the unknown:** "I don't know what will happen if I do it."

- **being a perfectionist:** "It's not quite right, I need more time to make it better."

- **it will take too long:** "I don't know when I'll have the time to do it."

- **not feeling qualified:** "Who would listen to me?"

Let's focus on how to overcome procrastination. How to use different ways, methods, and strategies to overcome whatever is stopping you from achieving your goals.

Begin by creating **SMART** goals: Specific Measurable Attainable Realistic Timely goals. Most people never finish their goals because they are too vague and there's no way to measure the progress. For example, let's use the common goal of trying to lose some weight:

the goal might be to lose 20 pounds. That gain of 20 extra pounds was not achieved overnight but yet people have a desire to instantly lose it overnight! When results are not instant and the realization hits that trying to lose the weight is going to take longer than they thought, they stop. The goal was not attainable, because the time to achieve the goal was not realistic. A better goal would be to lose 20 pounds in 6 months by eliminating sugars and soda, working out 20 minutes a day three times a week, and eating fruits and vegetables with every meal. An ant eats an elephant one bite at a time, and, in terms of achieving your success and your goals, so do you.

Write down your goal and then make it a **SMART** goal. Make it specific, what *exactly* is it you want to achieve; make it measurable, *when* will you achieve it by; and, most importantly, make it attainable by making it realistic. Don't say you're going to get up at 3 in the morning and run 10 miles if you've never run before, and certainly not if you don't normally wake up till 8 in the morning – that's not a realistic goal! The goal of being able to run 10 miles *can* be made realistic by breaking it down into smaller goals. Small goals equal little victories. Break the big goal down into smaller, stepping-stone goals and make each goal timely by beginning with something you can do within the scope of what you're doing now. Make changes one step at a time. Plan each step by writing it down and track your progress by recording every step you take.

Another way to overcome procrastination is to focus on the results, not the tasks you have to do. This means writing out your goals, then focusing on what those goals will bring into your life rather than focusing on what you have to do to achieve them. Take the focus away from yourself, it doesn't have to be all about you. Your successes can also help others to succeed. I love this verse from Jeremiah, Chapter 32.

> *[39] I will give them singleness of heart and action, so that they will always fear me for their own good and the good of their children after them.*

There are times when we will not move forward and we procrastinate because we think the only person we're hurting is ourselves. Once you realize what you're trying to achieve is about many other people, not just yourself, it may move you forward.

If you procrastinate because you're waiting for perfection, perfection will never come. People will often put off doing something because they want it to be perfect the first time. In Job 8:7 it says:

> *[7] Your beginnings will seem humble, so prosperous will your future be.*

This verse can be interpreted another way: Don't be upset about small beginnings because what you do later will be so much bigger than when you started. The things you're doing now, the little steps you're taking, will build and lead to bigger things but you have to be willing to take the first step. You have to be willing to move forward, and to start moving forward now.

Sometimes people procrastinate because they feel unqualified to do whatever it is they want to do. This is so untrue. There's no qualification required for dreaming and you don't need to be qualified to get started. In Isaiah 6: 5-7, Isaiah has been called upon by the

Lord to be a prophet but he feels unqualified and tries to explain by saying:

> *⁵ Then I said, "Woe is me for I am ruined! Because I am a man of unclean lips, and I live among a people of unclean lips; for my eyes have seen the King, the Lord of hosts."*

> *⁶ Then one of the seraphim flew to me with a burning coal in his hand, which he had taken from the alter with tongs.*

> *⁷ He touched my mouth with it and said, "Behold, this has touched your lips; and your iniquity is taken away and your sin is forgiven."*

You don't have to be perfect; you don't have to have all the answers. You just have to start. If you start moving forward, you will find there are people there who will assist you. As you keep going, you will *become* qualified, you will become an expert in the things you do by doing them. A number of people have become fitness experts after having been unfit and overweight themselves. Richard Simmons is one such person. He made a career as a fitness expert, yet at one point in his life he was tremendously obese. Through the process of battling his own weight issues and finding a way through his own challenges, he helped liberate millions of people. His VHS tapes, and I'm sure now DVDs, have sold millions of copies and his success has helped countless others to achieve their own. So what is it that you're not fighting through; what are you not doing that is supposed to help so many other people? It's not just your success. It is success for others.

Perhaps you're one of the many who procrastinate simply because it's going to take way too long. You never quite get started because whatever it is you need to do is going to take years to accomplish. I thought exactly that when I initially started speaking, but you may remember from an earlier chapter what Bill Bailey, one of my early mentors, told me about time: Man measures time by a clock but time is really a series of emotional experiences and the intensity of those emotions. So this means that if you want to accomplish something in a shorter period of time, you have to experience more each day, each week and each month. If you think something is going to take too much time, you procrastinate because you think you're never going to get it done. This can be overcome by simply experiencing more. To experience more you must do more, and you can do more by beginning to do it *now*.

Let's go back to the earlier goal of going for a 10 mile run. Clearly, if you're new to running, aiming to run 10 miles on your first attempt is absolutely unrealistic, but by simply breaking the ultimate goal down into smaller, more realistic goals, it becomes entirely achievable. However, if you currently workout only one day each week, the ultimate goal may seem a long way off. To beat procrastination and to shorten the process, begin to build in more experiences. In this case, adding just one more workout day to your week would instantly double your experience.

Call to Action: Overcome Procrastination

<u>Step One</u>: Commit to action, just say yes!

Say to yourself: I'm going to do this. I will be successful. I will achieve my goal.

<u>Step Two</u>: Break it down.

Break each big goal down into smaller, **SMART**, measurable goals, and write them down. Remember the value of writing things down from chapter Five.

<u>Step Three</u>: Tie your goals into daily activities.

Add new goals to your existing routines gradually. Make changes one step at a time so they fit around your current daily activities. Make a little bit of progress towards your goals each and every day. That way, they won't get away from you, and you won't look up 6 months from now and realize that you haven't moved forward.

CHAPTER SEVEN
ACCEPT THE CHANGE

Genesis, chapter 17 verse 5:

> *[17] No longer will you be called Abram; your name will be Abraham, for I have made you a father of many nations.*

Throughout the bible, especially in the old testament, there are many examples of where a person's name would change to signify the new person God had made them. A name had meaning, unlike today in modern society, where the name you're given is often a fashion statement or it happens to be special to your parents. Your name had meaning, so in order for you to become something new, God would change your name, and that change would signify who you were to become. In this case, in Genesis, Abraham, who did not have any children at the time, was told that he was going to be the father of many nations. This is something that didn't come true for a number of years, in fact his wife was almost 100 years old when they bore their first and only son Isaac, so the change in name happened many years before he saw the manifestation of God's promise.

When change occurs, you see the initial change, then watch the ripple effect. Case in point: November 9th 1989, the Berlin wall came down and it changed our whole world. For over 30 years there had been an East Berlin and a West Berlin and there had been a cold war to match it. In the blink of an eye, in terms of the life of our world, the whole world changed and there was a ripple effect; a whole nation changed and how industries dealt with each other changed, all because of one event. People who were enemies were now uneasy allies. Germany, which was divided into two nations, now became one. The great Soviet Union was no more. They, along with the Warsaw Pact, were now history. But, some people are still fighting and struggling with that change even 20 years later. No matter how big or small the change, you have to adjust to the new conditions. How are you going to walk through your change?

In order for you to achieve a better, more successful life, you have to accept and work through change. Change is constant. If you look back over your life, there is not a five year period that's the same. You might be the same height but you're a different weight. You may have changed professions, jobs, been promoted, been down-sized. You continue to change and you continue to evolve. We are made to change, and we will always continue to change while we are here. So how you think about change and how you adjust to the concept of change is important to you achieving success. In 1 Corinthians, Chapter 13, we are told:

> *11 When I was a child, I talked like a child, I thought*
> *like a child, I reasoned like a child. When I became*
> *a man, I put childish ways behind me.*

And that's what happens with us. We want to change, we want to go in a new direction, but we still try to do it being the same old person and that's not going to work. Just as Abraham couldn't be the father of nations as Abram, you can't have all the success you want for yourself as the person you are right now. You *will* go through change. Robert Louis Stevenson put it this way:

> *"Wherever we are, it is but a stage on the way to*
> *somewhere else, and whatever we do, however well*
> *we do it, it is only a preparation to do something*
> *else that shall be different."*
> *– Robert Louis Stevenson*

As you go through change, the way you think of success and what you identify as success will also change. The story of Paul Allen and Bill Gates is a perfect example. Some 30 or so years ago, Paul Allen met a young man two years younger than him at the Lakeside School. The man was Bill Gates. They were both into computer technology and the new technology was just coming into fashion at that time. I'm sure most people know that the two men went on to found the Microsoft Corporation but before that, Paul Allen dropped out of college. He was going to Washington and Bill Gates was going to Harvard, but Paul Allen convinced his friend to change his path and change his plan. Bill Gates had not planned on quitting college but Paul Allen showed him the upside to changing his plans. Gates and Allen made the change and the rest is history. As you know, both these men went on to become billionaires and create one of the largest corporations in the world.

Both Paul Allen and Bill Gates are on the 'Top 10' list of the wealthiest men in America, and certainly in the top 40 in the world – all because they were willing to change. But even more importantly, through the course of the change, they went from being young men with a passion; a passion for computer technology they wanted to bring to the world, to being men who ended up changing the world. They're both philanthropists now and work on projects to better the world. They changed as they went along, they continued to evolve. If asked, some thirty or forty years ago, if this was the course they saw set before themselves, the answer would have been absolutely not! Part of the fun is seeing not only what will change, but how you and things around you will change.

As you go through this process, you will start to see things differently and that's okay. What you *do* is going to become different, and that's okay too. In my own experience, I know as I started as a speaker, I started to look differently at things. TV shows that people still talked to me about were not shows I watched any more. I had watched them four or five years ago maybe but they didn't appeal to me any more. They didn't appeal because of where my heart and mind are *now*. This is something the Bible talks about. In Romans 12:2, it says,

² Do not conform any longer to the pattern of this world, but be transformed by the renewing of your mind. Then you will be able to test and approve what God's will is – his good, pleasing and perfect will.

Pastor Joel Osteen has learned how to deal with change. For 17 years he produced his father's television program at the Lakewood church. During this time, he was often asked by his father to deliver a message. Joel continued to push back, saying his job was behind the scenes. Finally, with his Dad in hospital, Joel was pressed into service. He delivered his first message a week before his father's passing. This was in 1999 and he has been teaching and ministering ever since. While it was unfortunate circumstances that caused the change to happen in Joel's life, the results of the change have been amazing. What was at the time of Joel's first message a 6,000 member ministry is now averaging more than 40,000 members attending each week. The television ministry is now seen in over 100 countries by 7 million viewers weekly. Although the initial change was painful for Joel and his family, as well as the Lakewood family, God had a plan to expand them. They moved from their original location to the old Compaq Center where the Houston Rockets used to play.

Keep in mind, part of the change process also changes your desires. Joel Osteen initially did not have a desire to minister the Gospel, Bill Gates initially had a desire to finish school. Each man recognized the change was for the better, and moved full steam ahead. Along the change highway, you will meet different people. Their job will be to help you change. Paul Allen met Bill Gates and they changed. People will come to you on this path and they will help facilitate your change, but it is important to remember you have to welcome the change. You can't stay who you are and expect to achieve what you want.

Take the apostle Peter. He was originally known as Simon as he walked with Jesus. Peter was originally a fisherman, called to be one of the original 12 apostles by Jesus. During his three years walking with Jesus, Peter went through many changes. He walked on water with Jesus, he was identified as 'The Rock' on which Jesus would build His ministry. But through all these changes, there was adversity, trial, and hard times. Peter was rebuked by Jesus for speaking out of turn; he denied knowing Jesus when Jesus was arrested. During the arrest, he cut a soldier's ear off. But through all these experiences, good and bad, Peter continued to grow into exactly what Jesus told him he would be, the cornerstone of the First Church.

Call to Action: Embrace the Change

First you must accept that you're going to experience anxiety as you go through change. Anxiety is a by-product of change. You can call it being uncomfortable, uneasy, out of your comfort zone. It is a break from your norm. Identify what you're feeling and journal those feelings each day. Writing down how you feel gives you a method to address these feelings. For example, you might write, "Worked out for two hours today, this is uncomfortable," or, "It's been six months of trying to get this new business contract, this is so frustrating, I feel like quitting, but I know it will work out." Whatever you write is okay. Look at what you write each day and then measure it against your goals. Measure how you feel against what you're aiming to achieve. This way, you can move through the change.

Next you must accept the change and commit to making the change. This can be done by using visualization; by remembering why you're doing this; by constantly looking at your goals, and using affirmations. These are all techniques you've been introduced to in previous chapters. Your affirmations are key. Repeat them every morning and every evening until, subconsciously, it becomes your will. Use your affirmations to accept the change and then continue to use them to *make* the change.

Put up visual reminders everywhere. If your idea of success is to have a larger home, find a picture of that home and pin it up on a wall where you'll see it every day. Use a dream-board. Dream-boards are incredible. They can help to facilitate the process and they can help to walk you through your change. Put up pictures on your board to act as reminders of everything you want to change in all aspects of your life. If you want more family time, put up pictures of families going on vacation; if you want a nice car, put up a picture of a nice car; if you want a large bank account, put up a picture that represents a large bank account to you; if you want to be spiritually closer to God, put up pictures of people worshiping and fellowship-ping. Put up pictures of whatever it is you want to pursue and put your dream-board somewhere prominent; put it where you'll see it day in and day out until one day you'll look up and realize that one-by-one you're achieving all of those dreams. Embrace the change, because whether you want it to or not, change is coming!

SECTION THREE
EXCELLENCE

In this section we learn how to walk in excellence in all that you do. By adopting new habits, and learning to give your best, you will grow more each day. Not to be mistaken for perfection, excellence must be proven by the trials you overcome. You learn these powerful lessons by experience and the people who teach and challenge you to strive for more.

CHAPTER EIGHT
GETTING BETTER
EVERY DAY

2 Chronicles, chapter 31 verses 20-21:

²⁰ *"This is what Hezekiah did throughout Judah, doing what was good and right and faithful before the Lord his God.*

²¹ *In everything that he undertook in the service of God's temple and in obedience to the law and the commands, he sought his God and worked whole-heartedly. And so he prospered.*

Hezekiah was the new king of Israel. Previous kings had fallen away from what was mandated, to biblically be obedient to the Lord. What Hezekiah did, was put together a systematic plan to serve God to the best of their ability. He cleaned out all of the temples abandoned by the previous kings. He promoted all of the priests to go back into the temples to consecrate themselves and then he reached out to the people. With places of worship solidified, he told his people they would worship God every single day; he told them who they were and what they were destined to do. But this was a gradual process and it took time to achieve.

> *"Excellence is a gradual result of all we strive to do better"*
> *– Pat Riley*

Hezekiah worked at it every single day with a single-minded focus and purpose. Eventually, he achieved his purpose and achieved it so well that the children of Israel were no longer cursed. He achieved it to the point that God was no longer angry with them; they were now blessed and walking in prosperity. One man made a conscious choice to walk in excellence; and the people he led were blessed for it.

The challenge for many people is we mistake excellence for perfection. The actual definition of excellence is:

Excellence > *noun* the quality of being excellent or the state of being exceptionally good.

Synonyms – distinction, merit, quality.

So excellence is not really perfection, excellence is the habits a person develops. This ties in with one of my favorite quotes of all time. When I first started speaking, this quote really drew me to it.

> *"We are what we repeatedly do. Excellence, therefore, is not an act but a habit"*
> *– Aristotle*

So again, it's not who we are, it's what we do every single day. One of the keys to achieving excellence is to realize that it's not perfection. The definition does not even have the word perfect in it. If you are trying to be perfect, you are setting yourself up for failure. In many situations that's exactly what we do, we try to be perfect in everything we do; we try this one attempt, one shot, make it perfect first time approach, and in doing so we stop ourselves from moving forward. Sir Laurence Olivier said this:

> *"Striving for perfection is the greatest stopper there is. You'll be afraid you can't achieve it...It's your excuse to yourself for not doing anything. Instead, strive for excellence, doing your best."*
> *– Sir Laurence Olivier*

That's the key. Strive to do your best, try every day and become a little bit better. In 2 Corinthians 8:7, it says:

> *[7] But just as you excel in everything – in faith, in speech, in knowledge, in complete earnestness and in your love for us – see that you also excel in this grace of giving.*

To me, this verse speaks of the balance in excellence. Don't strive to become excellent in just one area of your life, work to improve in all aspects of your life each and every day. I believe that's the true meaning of success. Let's look at Bill Bailey, my early mentor mentioned in a previous chapter. He is a Hall of Fame speaker and during his speaking career he also built a network organization that sold soap across 11 countries. He built his organization into a 64 million dollar a month business back in the 1970s. He did it by working every single day at improving the performance of his teams, consistently. Day in and day out, they made incremental improvements, until they were all excellent salespeople. Training took place constantly over the phone, since this was before the days of fax machines, PCs, laptops, and online conferences. The only way they could communicate was by phone and by snail mail; by writing letters using typewriters and creating carbon copies. Yet despite the period they worked in, he built a business many of us would be more than happy to have today.

He did it by treating his people well. He profit shared 25 per cent of the organization's profits with his team at the end of the year. That was a lot of dollars! His financial advisors spoke against giving his money away unnecessarily. But, he chose to do it that way because he wanted the best team and he wanted them to perform at their best every single day. Bill had the life; a private jet, a yacht, and he met the sitting Pope at the time, but he never forgot his humble beginnings. He has a big heart, and has supported programs to help others.

So, if excellence is what we do, let's look at one of my favorite athletes, and what he did, Olympian Edwin Moses. Edwin Moses had one of the most remarkable displays of excellence in the history of sports. He won every race he entered in his speciality, the 400 meter hurdles, for nine years, nine months, and nine days. Moses won a total of three Olympic medals, two gold and one bronze. He would probably have won a third gold medal, if not for the 1980 boycott. During the period from 1977 to 1987, Moses set four world records, won 107 finals and 122 races overall. He was known for his consistency: always taking 13 steps between each hurdle, and when other runners would start to tire, his gifts, training, and technique put him on top every time. Even though he has not competed since the 1988 Seoul Olympics, Edwin Moses still holds 26 of the 100 fastest times ever. The key to his excellence was striving to improve every day. He said this:

> *"I always had to keep improving my skills in order to remain competitive and keep winning."*
> – *Edwin Moses*

What are the things you need to do to achieve excellence in your life?

Call to Action: Do Your Best

First, decide to give your best every day. At the end of each day, measure your day and ask yourself: Did I give my best? If you are able to answer 'yes', what can you do tomorrow to get a little bit better? If you answer 'no', ask yourself: Why? What stopped me from doing my best today?

Once you figure out what's stopping you; what's slowing you down, write it in your journal. You must be very truthful with yourself when you consider your answers. After a period of 2 weeks, go back over your journal and review your answers. Is there a pattern of behavior stopping you from achieving the excellence you think you should? If you see a pattern developing, add an affirmation to change that behavior. For example, if you see a pattern of procrastination, create an affirmation that attacks procrastination.

I am a person who attacks my tasks first and foremost every day with high energy and with joy.

Henry Ford said this:

> *"Believe in your best, think your best, study your best. Have a goal for your best and never be satisfied with less than your best. Try your best and in the long-run, things will turn out for the best."*
> *– Henry Ford*

CHAPTER NINE
TRIALS BY FIRE

Isaiah chapter 48 verse 10:

> *¹⁰ See, I have refined you, though not as silver; I have*
> *tested you in the furnace of affliction.*

You will go through trials, you will go through tests, you will go through situations to see where you are and to get a measure of what you are able to accomplish. Trials are not sent to you by your enemy or made by misfortune or troubles, trials are there to make you better. This is one of my Dad's favorite quotes:

> *"The strongest steel is made in the hottest fire."*

If you don't believe that, take a look at the diamond. I find it pretty interesting that one of our most precious jewels is made through pressure and heat. Diamonds start out many miles beneath the surface of the earth as a piece of carbon. The sheer force exerted upon it by the weight of the earth, and the intense heat, squeezes the carbon, something that's fuel, into a precious stone. That sounds great for a piece of rock but what about us, what about how this works for us? Let's take a look at how pressure, from external forces or from competition, can bring out the best in a person.

Pete Sampras and Andre Agassi were two men constantly tested by each other. Both of them trained as teens with legendary tennis coach Nick Bollettieri. Pete Sampras won 14 grand slam titles, a record at the time, while Andre Agassi won 8, including the Career Grand Slam. Agassi won the Australian Open, the French Open, Wimbledon, and the US Open over his career while Sampras never won the French Open. In boxing, they say styles make fights. The same could be said of this tennis rivalry. Pete Sampras was the best serve and volley player of his era with a powerful serve and a powerful forehand. Andre Agassi was an excellent baseline player who had one of the most vicious returns of serve and an incredible backhand. They played each other 34 times, with Sampras winning 20 and Agassi 14. By themselves, both of them are considered two of the best tennis players ever. But without the fierce competition of their head-to-head matches, they may have never found out just how good they really were. Each man had to work through personal loss and injury as well as playing, or fighting, each other to become recognized as being the best in the world. You have to go through trials; go through competition, and go through challenges, in order to find out just how good you are. You need the trial of competition by fire to produce your best; otherwise you'll just sit in mediocrity wondering how good you could be.

One of my favorite plants is the giant sequoia tree. Also known as the Coast Redwood, giant sequoias are found in Central California in the Sequoia National Forest. They are the largest living organisms in the world, easily reaching heights of 300 feet and widths of well over 40 feet at the base. They're so big that you can actually create a two-way highway through a tree, that's pretty big! One of the interesting facts about sequoias is they actually help each other; they don't compete for resources. Instead, they create a huge root system that fuses them together and they *share* resources. In so doing, they also share their weight, creating stability for each tree by wrapping their roots together. Sequoias also have a remarkably thick skin – the bark can be 2 or 3 feet thick – and, something I find even more interesting, giant sequoias depend on fire for their survival.

Researchers studying sequoias found that the trees had stopped reproducing. This coincided with the fact that fires were being prevented from burning the giant sequoia groves. Through studies, they learned that the trees needed the fire in order to reproduce. It is in fact the heat of the fire that causes the pine cones to open up, allowing the seeds within to drop out as the fire burns through. This doesn't appear to make a lot of sense, burning a big tree in order to get the seeds out, but researchers found that giant sequoias are actually built to withstand fire. The thick bark – the thickest bark on earth – is made to resist fires. The sap also contains a fire retardant material which helps to prevent the fire from burning all the way through. They also found that sequoias can heal themselves over time. Studies of sequoias that had fallen, or been cut down, showed evidence of fires from centuries ago. The tree had burned and then regenerated itself, allowing it to survive for centuries. It literally healed itself like skin.

The giant sequoia needs fire and what's really interesting is that where fires have been hottest, clusters of giant sequoias have grown. They grow quickly but they need intense sunlight, so where fires have destroyed less resilient trees, sequoias flourish by dropping their seeds into the ashes. The fertile soil, water and sunlight provided perfect conditions for their growth: giant sequoias are, literally, built to reproduce in fire. We are the same way. We need the fire of trials to reproduce and to give our best.

Many times, without stress and without the pressure of needing to produce results, people turn out very mediocre results. We have to have that fire, that adversity, to put our best foot forward, to put our best effort out, and to achieve results we didn't think were possible. How many times, when faced with a deadline, have people miraculously come up with a great solution? That's because we need that fire, that trial, to achieve. Benjamin Franklin said this:

> *"To be thrown upon one's own resources, is to be cast
> into the very lap of good fortune. For our faculties
> then undergo a development and display an energy
> of which they were previously unsusceptible."*
> *– Benjamin Franklin*

Alex Rodriguez could tell you a little about overcoming adversity. For those of you who follow MLB baseball, you already know Rodriguez is the highest paid, and arguably the best, player in the game today. You also know he had the reputation of not being a clutch player. A clutch player is one who gets the big hit, makes the great defensive play and steals the base when the game is on the line. A clutch player does their best work in the toughest points of the game. Rodriguez, although recognized as great, was not seen as a clutch player: that title went to Derek Jeter, the man playing to his left in the field. But Alex Rodriguez wasn't satisfied with being just good, he wanted to be great. In baseball, being great means playing your best in the biggest games, the World Series. Well last year, 2009, he had his opportunity, and he didn't miss. ARod, as he is known, carried the Yankees in the playoffs and the World Series. He was the big bat in the line-up, the guy who had the big hits when they counted the most. When asked what changed, he couldn't really say, but I believe he has matured as a player. After going through adversity, he figured out how to adapt and overcome. The result? The Yankees won their 27th world title, the most in professional sports.

Overcoming trials is a necessary step to success. In James, Chapter 1, the Apostle James tells us:

> [2] *Consider it pure joy, my brothers, whenever you face trials of many kinds,*

> [3] *Because you know that the testing of your faith develops perseverance.*

> [4] *Perseverance must finish its work so that you may be mature and complete, not lacking anything.*

James is telling us we must develop perseverance, and the only way to truly build the strength to overcome your challenges is to go *through* the tough times. There are no shortcuts to this process. You cannot depend on the experiences of others to guide you through. These are lessons you must learn the old fashioned way, by taking them for what they are; medicine for the success minded person.

Call to Action: Become Fire Proven

Turn your adversity to your advantage. Change your perspective. The challenges you face are actually here to make you better. Shift your mind-sight to recognize the opportunity in the adversity. Look beyond the pain and the discomfort and focus on the goal. Start to look and see things in a different way. Start to see the advantages of the trial and of the challenges that you're going through. Use your past victories to propel you forward. Recognize the adversity you've already overcome in your past. Decide today you are a sequoia, you thrive in the hottest fires.

Write down in your journal the details of previous trials you've had. Record how you felt when you were in the middle of those trials and then how you felt when you made it through. You came through those fires. Recognize that you will not only survive, but you will thrive in your current fires.

CHAPTER TEN
MENTORS

Matthew chapter 4 verses 1-3:

> *¹ Then Jesus was led by the spirit into the desert to be tempted by the devil.*

> *² After fasting for forty days and forty nights, he was hungry.*

> *³ The tempter came to him and said, "If you are the son of God, tell these stones to become bread."*

In this scripture in Mathew, Jesus Christ had just been baptized by John the Baptist. The heavens had opened up and a dove had appeared. The voice of God said, "This is my son in who I am well pleased." So he had just been promoted, but immediately after being promoted his mentor, the Holy Spirit, led him into a trial. Jesus was led into a challenge to test him and to see if he was ready.

> *When the student is ready, the teacher will appear.*
> *– Buddhist Proverb*

Mentorship is critical to your future success. We all need mentors and mentors can assist us in a number of ways. One, they have experience. They've been there and they've done that, and they've done it successfully so they can help us cut down the number of errors we might make as we go through the process of figuring out how we're going to achieve a result. Two, they have the knowledge. They understand where you are and where you have to go because they've already been there themselves. They recognize the adversity you're going to face, they know the pitfalls, they know the challenges, they understand the process, and they can help eliminate some of those processes, helping to accelerate the learning curve. Three, they accelerate your learning curve. A mentor can help us to get through challenges at an accelerated pace and also give us a hyper velocity to go beyond the pitfalls and challenges facing us, allowing us to accelerate to a whole new level.

Mentors also push us beyond our comfort zone. They are there to challenge us to do more than we thought possible. With a mentor, you may even achieve results you never knew you had in you. A great example of a mentor is Mia Redrick, my book coach. It's because of Mia that you're actually reading this book. She made this book a reality for me because of her expertise, her connections, and her drive. By showing me a process to follow, then working with me and helping me to overcome my own personal fearstorms, obstacles, and self-limiting beliefs, she made this book possible. Mia is an accomplished author in her own right. Her book *Time for mom-Me* showed me what was possible for my book, and her own personal experience made her understanding of the process invaluable. Mia was an incredible coach and mentor to me and without such a mentor in my life, this book may have never been possible.

A mentor can also give you access to people you have never met before. In my case, and in the case of my businesses, I met people like Bill Bailey, a man who greatly influenced my life, and Les Brown and Willie Jolley, both world renowned international speakers, because of connections made through mentors. Meeting people like Bob Yates, Bernie Dorman, and Dr. Jeff Magee provides not only an opportunity to learn but also an opportunity to grow from the experience. Mentorship is critical to accelerating your success.

> *"At the end of the road I will be happy. Happy knowing that I lived my dreams and not my fears! Happy that I trusted God and surrendered to his plan. Happy that I lived life on purpose and left my legacy. I will truly be happy that I helped so many others to do the same."*
> – Bob Yates, Circle of Champions

Mentorship also creates the taught-teach pattern. Once you're taught by a mentor, it's then incumbent on you to teach the next generation after you. So, once mentored, you become the mentor. This is a thread that can be found connecting many successful people. For example, Bill Bailey mentored Jim Rohn, Les Brown, Tony Robbins, Dr. Stan Harris, and many others. Les Brown then mentored Willie Jolley, Bob Yates, and many others. Willie Jolley and Bob Yates have mentored me, and now I mentor small business owners, young men, and people who are tired of mediocrity and striving to achieve success. The people I mentor will then go on to mentor others in their own right. In 1 Corinthians 4: 15-17, it says:

> *15 Even though you have ten thousand guardians in Christ, you do not have many fathers, for in Christ Jesus I became your father through the gospel.*
>
> *16 Therefore I urge you to imitate me.*
>
> *17 For this reason I am sending to you Timothy, my son whom I love, who is faithful in the Lord. He will remind you of my way of life in Christ Jesus, which agrees with what I teach everywhere in every church.*

The Apostle Paul is telling the church of Corinth: You have a lot of people around you but you don't have mentors, so what I'm going to do is send a mentor, a person that I know is going to teach you the right way and show you how to achieve these results. How to walk this walk the right way.

To me, what we learn from Paul, and what becomes critical in life, is that we have to find the *right* mentor. You have to find a person who can teach you the right way. Just because a mentor is mentoring someone you know, it doesn't mean they're a right fit for you. To be a fit, you need someone with the same DNA as yourself – the same mindset and the same mind-sight. You also need to be able to receive that person's feedback. No matter how great they are, if the information comes at you in a way that you can't receive it and digest it, it's a waste; a waste to the mentor and to you.

> *"I wish for you a life of wealth, health and happiness; a life in which you give to yourself the gift of patience, the virtue of reason, the value of knowledge."*
> *– Jim Rohn*

The mentor you choose must have the correct intentions. In some cases, a mentor will charge you, in others they may not. I've had mentors who charged me a nominal monthly fee and others who did not, either way is fine. It really comes down to where you are in life and where you want to go; what you want to achieve. I think it's fair to say that sometimes the lessons that cost you the most, financially and otherwise, are the lessons you learn best.

Looking for the common thread can also help you to identify the right mentor for you. For example, Columbia University professor Dr. Benjamin Graham mentored a young man named Warren Buffet. Warren Buffet mentored Bill Gates and a baseball superstar named Alex Rodriguez. Do you see the thread? Each person is considered to be one of the best in the field they work in. Warren Buffet in stocks, Bill Gates in computer software, and Alex Rodriguez in baseball.

In 1 Samuel 9:7 it says:

> [7] *Saul said to his servant, "If we go, what can we give the man. The food in our sacks is gone. We have no gift to give to the man of God. What do we have?"*

Samuel was a prophet, he was a man who was giving information so he was a mentor. Those who talked to him wanted to give him a gift, highlighting the fact that sometimes mentoring is going to cost you. With or without cost, it's crucial that the mentor you choose has *your* best interests at heart. Novelist Thomas Wolfe once said this of a publisher who saw potential in his work:

> *"I was sustained by one piece of inestimable good fortune. I had for a friend a man of immense and patient wisdom and a gentle but unyielding fortitude. I think that if I was not destroyed at this time by the sense of hopelessness which these gigantic labours had awakened in me, it was largely because of the courage and the patience of this man. I did not give in because he would not let me give in."*
> *– Thomas Wolfe*

That is the essence of what a mentor can do. A mentor can help you through your trials and help you find a way through your challenges.

Call to Action: Identify Your Needs

Identify desires or needs for your mentor to work on. What is it that you need the most? What do you need to do; what do you need to accelerate quickly to achieve your success? In James 4:2, it says:

> *2 Ye have not because ye ask not. KJV*

So ask what you need. Identify what your needs are and then write them down. Concentrate on three areas of your life, identify your needs in each area, then write down the needs that, if met, would most change your life in each area. Make a verbal agreement with yourself to find a mentor for each one of those areas. I have mentors in many areas of my life. I have mentors who teach me and challenge me to grow, and I thank God each and every day for the incredible men and women who have been brought into my life to help me achieve the success that I see is destined for me.

Call to Action: Read Success Stories

Read the biographies of successful people. Look at the people who have influenced the lives of successful people and look for patterns; look for the common threads. You'll always find a common thread in the mentorship of people who succeed. Start to look for that same thread among the people who are already in your life. As you look for those threads, you'll find the right mentor; you'll find the right person to take you in the right direction to find your own success.

SECTION FOUR
DETERMINATION

In this section we discuss the importance of determination. How becoming mentally tough, focused, and tenaciously committed to becoming all you were destined to be is critical to success. Along the way, you'll learn the importance of experiencing failure, the right attitude, and how overcoming obstacles are all a part of the determined path to your greatness.

CHAPTER ELEVEN
MENTAL TOUGHNESS

Proverbs chapter 4 verses 25-27:

> [25] *Let your eyes look straight ahead, fix your gaze directly before you.*

> [26] *Make level paths for your feet and take only ways that are firm.*

> [27] *Do not swerve to the right or the left; keep your foot from evil.*

Mental toughness is resistance training for your mind. Men and women who workout with weights are using resistance training to strengthen their bodies. Resistance training helps them to increase the strength of their muscles and skeletal system; to develop a stronger frame, and to become able to withstand more stress and more pressure. The same thing happens with our minds. We can train our minds by taking them through a resistance training course.

> *"Let me tell you a secret that has led me to my goal.*
> *My strength lies solely in my tenacity."*
> *– Louis Pasteur*

The great beauty of resistance training for the mind is that *everyone* can increase their mental toughness, everyone can improve their mental strength. A good example of this comes from my days in grade school. In math, we were timed on our additions, subtractions, division and multiplication time tables. We were given two minutes to answer 20 questions. That became two minutes to answer 50 questions and then it became only one minute to answer 50 questions. By doing this, our minds became increasingly rapid at processing numbers; we were building our mental abilities.

The same thing happens in every area of your mind when you apply resistance training. Champion golfer Tiger Woods is another great example. As a youngster, he had his father make loud noises around him during his golf training sessions. His father would move around, rustle papers, drop his golf bag, and do all kinds of different things to cause distractions. Through this process, Tiger Woods learned how to maintain his concentration. He used resistance training to strengthen his mental discipline.

"I am the toughest golfer mentally."
– Tiger Woods

Think of your mind as a muscle and, just like any other muscle in your body, it must be developed and consistently exercised to prevent atrophy. When atrophy occurs in muscles, they wither away. When atrophy occurs in your mind, you lose your mental skill.

An interesting example of the power of this sort of mental discipline can be found in the stories of American football players Ryan Leaf and Peyton Manning. In the 1998 NFL draft, Peyton Manning was drafted number one and Ryan Leaf was drafted number two. Both of these men were outstanding players and at the time there was a huge amount of publicity surrounding who would be picked number one. Either way and with either player, it was a win-win situation for the choosing teams. The Indianapolis Colts had the first pick and they decided to go with Peyton Manning. The San Diego Chargers had the second pick and they went with Ryan Leaf. Since that day in 1998, Peyton Manning has started in all 192 games of his pro career; he's thrown 366 touchdowns, 181 interceptions, and he's been sacked 215 times. Ryan Leaf on the other hand, made only 21 starts in 25 games, threw 14 touchdowns, 36 interceptions, and was sacked 65 times. Peyton Manning has appeared in two Super Bowls and won one, and he's been a league MVP (most valuable player) four times. Ryan Leaf was out of pro football by the time he was 25 years old. So what created the difference between these two players? Mental toughness.

Peyton Manning had a mental game that far surpassed Ryan Leaf's game. He had a maturity and an intensity about him; a single-minded focus and determination to succeed. He studied for hours. He worked tirelessly throughout the pre-season and the off-season to become better at his craft. Even today, as accomplished as he is, he works in the off-season with his wide receivers, throwing patterns to them; countless patterns, time after time, so that their movements and timings become subconscious. That way, when the pressure is on in competition, they don't even have to think about it, it's all done. They're all doing the right thing at the right time, and they're all on the same page. That is what marks the difference between a future Hall of Famer and a person who is a trivial pursuit question now.

> *"Some guys need to see it on a grease board...I like when you can see it in your mind."*
> *– Peyton Manning*

The key is to learn to focus. A light can light up a room but you can also take that same light, apply focus to it, and it can cut metal as a laser. So it's all about focus. A memorable example of mental focus can be found in Kerri Strug. In 1996, Kerri Strug was on the US women's gymnastics team competing in the Atlanta Olympics. Although not particularly well-known, she had already won a team bronze medal in the 1992 Barcelona Olympics. The 1996 women's gymnastics team was expected to bring home gold, competing on home territory, but Kerri wasn't expected to play a major role.

The vault was the last exercise in the team competition. Two of the more famous gymnasts in the US team had already taken their vault and fallen. This meant that all of a sudden Kerri, who hadn't been expected to perform at a high level, was needed, and she needed to produce the performance of her life to keep the team's hopes of a gold medal alive. She took her first vault but as she landed, she felt a snap in her ankle. It wasn't realized at the time, but she had actually severely sprained her ankle and torn two ligaments. As she walked away from the vault, she was limping noticeably but her coach, unsure of the points difference between the US team and the closely matched Russian team, turned to her and said, "We need you to take one more vault." If you saw it at the time, or if you've seen it since on video (you can see it on YouTube) you'll remember that moment. The moment Kerri made her decision is clearly visible. Her face changed; it became very calm and it became totally focused. Only 18 years old and 4 foot 10 inches tall, she stepped up to take her second vault. She was so focused that there was no sign of a limp on her run up and after her vault she landed perfectly on that busted ankle. She heard it snap again but she lifted it up and turned around to present herself to the judges. Only then; only after completing her task, did she collapse to the ground. Her pain was so great that she actually had to crawl off of the mat.

It was discovered later that Kerri's second vault was in fact not needed and the coach faced heavy criticism but that's not the point. Here was a young woman with a goal. Her goal was to get the gold medal for the US team and she realized that to achieve her goal, she was going to have to work through her pain; she was going to have to overcome the obstacle facing her, and she had to find a way to get the job done for her team-mates and for herself and she did it. *That* is laser focus.

> *"The first law of success is concentration. To bend all the energies to one point, to go directly to that point looking neither to the left nor the right."*
> *– William Mathews*

If you want to become strong mentally, you must learn how to focus your mind. You must learn how to exercise your mind and how to focus on one single point to achieve.

Call to Action: Mental Exercise

James 1:8

> [8] *He is a double-minded man, unstable in all he does.*

You have to be focused; you have to prevent your mind from being all over the place, so how do you do this? Begin by setting up some easy wins and work towards increasing the intensity. Start with simple but effective mind exercises such as brushing your teeth with your left hand if you're right-handed, or vice-versa. Break the patterns your mind has developed over the years. For example, without realizing it, you probably always tie your shoes in a set order; try tying your shoes differently. You probably have a set route that you drive to get to the store; drive a different route. You have to exercise your mind differently to make it think differently. Try learning something new. My son Andrew is on the chess team in school and chess is something I always wanted to learn, so now we're learning chess together and it's making me think differently. Always strive to find new ways to challenge yourself.

Call to Action: Physical Exercise

A healthy vessel is needed for a healthy mind. Your mind is constantly bombarded by negative thoughts and stress. If you don't have a regular exercise routine, you're not going to be able to deal with that stress. Adopt a regular exercise routine. Just like your mental exercise routine, start slowly and work your way up. Set up easy wins first then continue to push yourself physically. This will give you confidence that you can handle more mentally than you thought possible.

I have a good friend who five years ago would not run at all. Today, she's running half-marathons and running 5ks regularly. This is an incredible physical change but her mental approach to running has also become totally different. In the past, she always struggled to keep herself in shape and in a physical condition she felt happy with. Now, if she loses a bit of condition, she just says she'll get it back by going out and doing a bit more running. Exercise changes your whole approach. Learn to exercise yourself physically and mentally in order to get the results you need.

CHAPTER TWELVE
FAILURE IS YOUR TEACHER

Luke chapter 5 verses 4-7:

> *4 When he had finished speaking, he said to Simon, "Put out into deep water, and let down the nets for a catch."*

> *5 Simon said, "Master, we've worked hard all night and haven't caught anything. But because you say so, I will let down the nets."*

> *6 When they had done so, they caught such a large number of fish that their nets began to break.*

> *[7] So they signaled their partners in the other boat to come and help them, and they came and filled both boats so full that they began to sink.*

Failure is a valuable teacher. In this example, Simon, later called Peter, is an experienced fisherman. Jesus was trained as a carpenter, which is far from being a commercial fisherman. So when he gave the instruction to Simon to go out into the water and to cast his nets again, Simon knew it was not the best way to catch fish. He knew that fish come to the top of the water at night to feed because the water is cooler; he knew that during the day they go deeper to avoid being exposed to predators in the daylight. He also knew that it was now morning, the heat of the day was already on the water, and they'd already failed in that same spot, so it made no sense to try again. But, because Jesus told him to do it, Simon did. By following the instruction of Jesus, they pulled in a catch the likes of which they'd never seen before. The catch was so great they had to bring in other boats; there were so many fish, their nets were tearing. That is the power of following the word of Christ.

What we learn from this, and what I'd like to focus on in this chapter, is that failure can be a great teacher for you.

> *"Entrepreneurs experience on average 3.8 failures before final success. What sets the successful ones apart is their amazing persistence. There are a lot of people out there with good and marketable ideas but pure entrepreneurial types almost never accept defeat."*
> *– Lisa M. Amos*

If you haven't failed, it's because you haven't tried anything. You have to get out there and become comfortable with the fact that there are times where you will miss the mark if you want to become a success. You have to learn from your mistakes and you have to get your mistakes quickly out of the way so you can try again. You can't fear failure, quite the opposite, you have to embrace it. One of the key differences between successful and unsuccessful people is that unsuccessful people fear failing; they fear trying, because there may be a chance of failing. But successful people understand that there's a lesson in their failure. Michael Jordan said this:

> *"I've missed more than 9000 shots in my career. I've lost almost 300 games. 26 times, I've been trusted to take the game winning shot and missed. I've failed over, and over, and over again in my life. And that is why I succeed."*
> *– Michael Jordan*

You have to become comfortable with failure because failure is the incubator for success. Let's take a toddler for example. A toddler's first stage of moving is crawling. Not satisfied, they're already trying to reach the next stage; they're trying to walk. They try to get up on their feet, and they fall over and over. How many times will the baby fall down before it takes one or two weak tottering steps? They fall but they immediately get up again. They fail but they try again. What I find interesting is that as parents, we don't try to stop them from falling down; in fact we encourage them to try, knowing they will fall again. We do this because we know the more they fall, the quicker our children will walk.

Somewhere along the line we become afraid of falling down. As we become adults we develop a fear of failure, and we become unable to rise back to our original levels quickly after a fall. We need to recapture the same drive for success that we had as toddlers. Children have a natural drive and intensity in their approach to getting to the next level. They don't just learn, they immerse themselves in the task until they're good at it. They have no fear of failure. My son Andrew has that kind of focus in everything he tries. When he tried martial arts, he quickly rose to a purple belt. When he tried chess, he learned quickly. He plays chess so well; he's reached the point where I'm not looking forward to playing him! It's the same with video games and with football, anything he learns, he learns with the same focus; he wants to get right at it, and he's not afraid of failing.

Thomas Edison was someone who had the same approach to life and his work. Edison invented something we now use every single day, the light bulb filament. He is often given credit with the invention of the light bulb but in fact the light bulb already existed. However, the bulbs of the time only lasted about 40 hours before burning out and Thomas Edison's invention was a light bulb filament that lasted a great deal longer, up to 1500 hours. We know he had at least 2000 failed attempts before he finally found the right material. Edison was continually questioned about his repeated attempts and subsequent failures by reporters. When asked about all his failures he said this:

> *"I have not failed. Not once. I've just found 10,000 ways that didn't work."*
> *– Thomas A. Edison*

This speaks to his mindset. He realized that if something didn't work, he had to just move on and try the next thing. Every successful sales person has the same approach. They keep going; they look for the next "no" so they can get to the next "yes." As a project manager, there were times I had to have a plan A, B, and C...sometimes getting a lot further down the alphabet than I wanted...before the answer was found! But I've always believed that once we found out something didn't work, it was one less thing we had to worry about.

In Proverbs 24:16, it says:

> [16] *For though a righteous man falls seven times, he rises again, but the wicked are brought down by calamity.*

The Bible teaches us that a good man will keep trying to rise. He will always get up and continue to go forward. Take for example Lee Iacocca. Lee Iacocca was fired unceremoniously from his position as President of the Ford Motor Company by then Chairman Henry Ford II. Iacocca was the creative force behind the legendary Ford Mustang, the Lincoln Continental Mark III, the Mercury Cougar, and the Mercury Marquis, yet despite these successes, he was fired in 1978; a year in which Ford posted a profit of 2 billion dollars.

But a good man always gets back up, and Iacocca was courted by Chrysler. At the time, the Chrysler Corporation's situation was a little different than Ford. Chrysler was broke. They had no money for new projects, they were losing millions of dollars quarterly, losing market share and morale was very low. Chrysler was a mess. However, Iacocca saw it as an opportunity, a chance to paint on a new canvas; to have full autonomy to go in and to change the culture, something Iacocca always wanted to do at Ford. First, he worked with the federal government to stabilize the company by securing low interest loans. Meanwhile he went to work on changing the culture. Not long after he took over Chrysler in the early 80s, K-cars and minivans started coming off the assembly line. These were projects he wanted to do at Ford, but couldn't get them through. Next, he purchased AMC (the American Motors Corporation) so he could bring the Jeep line, particularly the Cherokee, to Chrysler. His boldness, drive, and desire turned Chrysler around. He took a company that was on the brink of failure and made a strong, innovative organization. Chrysler became a place where people were proud to come to work. He didn't look at the failure; he looked at the future and the potential for success. Lee Iacocca said this about failure:

> *"So what do we do? Anything. Something. So long as we don't just sit there. If we screw it up, start over. Try something else. If we wait until we've satisfied all the uncertainties, it may be too late."*
> *– Lee Iacocca*

Remember this; the best in the world fail most of the time. Derek Jeter is considered a Hall of Fame caliber hitter in baseball but he makes an out, or fails, 7 out of 10 times.

Call to Action: Start Failing Now

Write down all of the ideas you recently tried and failed, or you haven't attempted because you're afraid of failing. For example, have you tried to lose weight? Have you tried to exercise more? Or have you been thinking of making a career change but not started looking? Instead of not trying again, get started right now. How do you know it won't work? You can't know the outcome until you try! Adopt a new approach to failure. If trying leads to failing then do something different and try it again. Learn from your failure; get together with your mentor in the area you're having trouble in and figure out where and why you missed the mark. Write out all of the reasons you identify. By the end of this process, you will have a list of the thoughts and actions that led to you missing the mark. You'll have a how-to guide to make the corrections; you'll have a blueprint for your future success.

Call to Action: Learn to Accept the Lesson in the Failure

Accept failure for what it really is. A failure is a lesson in disguise. Adjust your mindset to see failure as a required step towards success. Take your notes from the last exercise and study them. Make a note in your journal of where, why, and how you failed, along with the adjustments you need to make. Review your notes weekly. If you follow these steps, you will have different results; you will have a different attitude to failure.

CHAPTER THIRTEEN
ATTITUDE

Proverbs chapter 13 verse 15:

> [15] *A happy heart makes the face cheerful, but heart-ache crushes the spirit.*

Your attitude. It's critical to your success. There's no escaping the fact that stuff is going to happen. It is a reality of life. You're going to have challenges. Computers are going to break, cars are going to fail to start, kids are going to be sick, you're going to be planning a project and things are just not going to work right – stuff happens!

The difference between a successful person and an unsuccessful person is how they choose to respond to the situation. Your attitude is the incredible driving force toward success or towards failure.

> *"Optimism is the faith that leads to achievement.*
> *Nothing can be done without hope and confidence."*
> *– Helen Keller*

The great news is that *you* have the ability to choose which attitude *you* are going to have. In Hebrew 12:15, it says:

> [15] *See to it that no one misses the grace of God and that no bitter root grows up to cause trouble and defile many.*

Attitudes can be good or bad. Attitudes can be taught, or handed down from one person to another; you may have been taught, without realizing it, how to respond to certain situations. As I watched the 2010 Vancouver Winter Olympics on television, it occurred to me how much attitudes can change. When I was a young man during the cold war, we were taught that the Soviet Union was the big bad bear, so much so that we would mentally 'boo' every time the Russians performed in the Olympics. An iconic moment in Olympic history occurred in 1980 when the US ice hockey team beat the Soviet Union team, considered to be the best team in the world at the time, in a match that became known as the "Miracle on Ice." The US team did go on to win Olympic gold but the Miracle on Ice was in fact only a medal-round game, not the final. The actual final, played against Finland, seems virtually forgotten, but everybody old enough in America remembers the big win against the Soviet Union. This was because of our collective attitude as a nation: the Soviet Union was bad and we were good. Times have changed. Today, the

Russian Federation and the US are trading partners. It's the same people; but our attitude is different.

Attitudes, good or bad, can also be nurtured through your environment and the people around you. Be aware of the television shows you watch, the newspapers, books, and magazines you read, the music you listen to, and the conversations you have on a daily basis. You must recognize you are always in a position of learning and everything you ingest, everything you take into your system, stays there. I heard an interesting statistic recently relating to the information we receive or expose ourselves to on a daily basis; a survey revealed that only 3 per cent of the participants monitor the data they receive day in and day out which means that 97 per cent are simply exposing themselves to and receiving whatever is being sent. Be conscious of your everyday environment and be aware that the information you're exposing yourself to has a direct effect on your attitude.

Being around negative people will promote a bad attitude. If you're around negative people, find new people. Negative people will carry you down; you need people around you with a growth mindset, people who will help you to grow; help you to get to where you're going, and to achieve all you've been promised. A great example of a negative personality is Eeyore, the donkey in the classic Winnie the Pooh children's stories. That donkey had some challenges! He certainly didn't see the world through rose-colored glasses, everything was negative and he even talked that way. He had a negative view to everything in life and it showed; the glass was half-empty in every situation he went through. This character demonstrates how important it is to be aware of how you feel about yourself. Self-pity promotes a bad attitude.

We have to be aware of bad attitudes and the influences that can bring our attitude down. D.H. Lawrence said this:

> "I never saw a wild thing sorry for itself. A small bird will drop frozen dead from a bough without ever having felt sorry for itself."
> – D.H. Lawrence

Positive influences can help create a positive attitude. A positive mental attitude can be the difference between whether you make it or fail. With a positive mental attitude, you are able to see obstacles as opportunities, and challenges as chances to excel. By having a positive mental attitude, you attract like-minded people into your life. You draw the people toward you who can give you the assistance you need to accomplish your goals.

I have continually worked on my attitude and I believe it has been critical to my success. On a daily basis, I try hard to repel any negative thoughts and to limit negative input into my system. In the IT world there's an acronym GIGO which stands for garbage in, garbage out.

GIGO = Garbage In, Garbage Out

In other words, what you ingest, what you take in, is eventually what comes out of you. I think this is very true. If you eat fast food every single day, you know what's going to happen to you physically. So what happens to you when you "eat" bad food mentally every single day? The psychological manifestations are very real. Negative input leads to a negative attitude, which equals poor or little result at all.

Symptoms include unhappiness, a sense of despair, self-pity, and an overall feeling of being unsuccessful.

On the other hand, adopting a positive mental attitude is like super charging your body. A positive approach to life lets you operate at a whole new level of intensity. You see things differently; you view success differently, and your mind-sight changes to let you see things clearly. You begin to see the opportunities that may previously have passed you by. A positive attitude gives you an avenue to access those opportunities. People with positive attitudes are drawn to you. Your attitude is a cologne that will attract or repel people. Make sure you're attracting the right ones. It's critical to your success that you monitor your attitude and that you are prepared to *change* your negative attitudes for the better.

> *"If you don't like something, change it; if you can't*
> *change it, change the way you think about it."*
> *– Mary Engelbreit*

To me, there is no can't. If you take the word "can't" out of your mental dictionary you will see the world differently. There may be a, "can't right now," or, "I don't understand how to achieve it right this second," but there is never a, "can't achieve it."

When I talk in schools and universities, I always tell them there is no can't. On one occasion, a kid questioned me by saying, "Well, you can't be an astronaut." Well, sure you can! Richard Branson and others like him are already working on public space flight projects. If you have enough money, you *can* get on one of these spaceships and you *can* go into space. So, in theory, you *can* become an astronaut if that is your true goal. It's all about your attitude. When you think positively, doors begin to open and opportunities become available to you.

> *"Opportunity is a parade. Even as one chance passes, the next is a fife and drum echoing in the distance."*
> – Robert Brault

Call to Action: Create a Successful Attitude

Proverb 23:7

> [7] *For as he thinks within himself, so is he.*

I'm not promising that this exercise will make you feel better, but it *will* help you to manage your attitude, regardless of your feelings. This is important because many times we allow ourselves to be led by our feelings as opposed to us managing our feelings.

The first thing you must do is *decide* to have a positive attitude. Make that choice. Make that decision and commit to it. Challenge yourself to look for the good in tough situations. This is going to feel strange at first and you may even feel like you're some kind of a fake, that you're not very authentic, and that you're lying to yourself, but keep pressing ahead. Understand what it is you're doing and why you're doing it; you're rewriting years of mental programming. You have to erase all the existing bad tape before you can write new tracks on that tape, so it's going to take you some time.

But remember what Bill Bailey said about time!

How much time really depends on you but to help accelerate the process, be very aware of the information you're feeding into yourself. Change your pattern. Look for positive books, magazines, and newspapers to read, listen to positive music, and engage only in positive conversations. If a conversation becomes negative, either stop the conversation by politely changing the subject or nicely walk away. Do not get yourself tied up in gossip, back-biting, negative thoughts, or general complaining about situations, walk away from all of those conversations.

Tell your good friends and your family members that you're working on your attitude and you're monitoring your language. Ask them to help you by lovingly correcting you as you go through these changes. Your job is to remain open to receiving the correction. I often correct myself in mid sentence when I hear the words I'm saying and realize they're not representative of the man I believe myself to be; they're not reflecting who I am. *I* get to decide who I am because I've heard from God, and I know, what I'm destined to be. *You* can change your attitude by changing your language and changing your thinking.

Call to Action: Create Attitude Affirmations

There's a particular song from the 1980s that I always remember. It was sung by Mathew Wilder and some of the lyrics were …"ain't nothing gonna break my stride, nobody's gonna slow me down, oh no, I got to keep on moving. Ain't nothing gonna break my stride, I'm running and I won't touch the ground, oh no, I got to keep on moving…"

Back then, I'd sing this song to myself all the time; even as I think of it now, I can hear it playing in the background of my mind. I didn't realize it at the time but I was actually programming my mind; learning how to persevere and how to strengthen myself through tough times.

I was in the military and as I was going through adversity and challenges. This song was constantly on the radio and I remember humming it to myself and finding it was strengthening me. The lyrics became an affirmation for me. Make your own attitude affirmations. Create positive affirmations relating to the areas of your life you're changing and make a commitment to yourself to adopt the change. For example, an affirmation may be: I'm a positive person; I'm a person who speaks positive messages of life. I only see the good in people. Those who are negative are not a part of my life. One I often use is: "I bring light and joy into the lives of everyone I touch. I am a man of God and in every room I walk into, I bring the light of Jesus with me. Jesus is my source and my King."

Call to Action: Change Your Environment

Add flowers. Put positive images in the spaces where you spend most of your time. Be aware of what you're listening to and what's going on around you. Monitor the shows you watch on television.

I personally, do not watch the news in the evening. I refuse to go to bed with negative, destructive images playing in my mind as I close my eyes and go to sleep. Those images, if the last thing I saw, would become written into my subconscious. If you watch TV, make it positive TV. Be very aware of the information you're feeding into your mind. Remember GIGO. Make a conscious effort to change your environment and to create a completely positive environment for a period of 30 days. Track the information you're taking in for one month, make adjustments and watch what happens. Watch what people around you start to say about your attitude and about how you carry yourself.

These changes are incremental, they need to be made one step at a time. Remember, Rome wasn't built in a day, so cut yourself a break, give yourself an opportunity to grow into the new you, and be positive about your results; *expect* great results.

CHAPTER FOURTEEN
OVERCOMING OBSTACLES AND CIRCUMSTANCES

Numbers chapter 13 verses 30-33:

> *30 Then Caleb silenced the people before Moses and said, "We should go up and take possession of the land, for we can certainly do it."*

> *31 But the men who had gone up with him said, "We can't attack those people; they are stronger than we are."*

> *32 And they spread among the Israelites a bad report about the land they had explored. They said, "The*

*land we explored devours those living in it. All the
people we saw there are of great size.*

[33] *We saw the Nephilim there (the descendants of Anak
came from the Nephilim). We seemed like grasshoppers in our own eyes, and we looked the same to
them."*

In this scripture, Moses had received instruction from the Lord to
send people into the promised land to scout it out. He sent in twelve
people, and when they came back from scouting the land, the Bible
says two of them, Caleb and Joshua, gave a good report, but ten of
them gave a poor or a bad report. The two were saying, let's take
this land, God is on our side and we can do it, but the other ten men
were saying no. They didn't believe that taking the land was even a
possibility and they believed that the giant Nephilim would see them
as nothing but grasshoppers. It was an obstacle; it was a challenge.
Ten of them clearly didn't want to step up to the challenge but the
other two were all ready to jump into the middle of it.

> *"The difference between the impossible and the pos-
> sible lies in a man's determination."*
> *– Tommy Lasorda*

Most of the time, that's the problem we face. As soon as an obstacle
pops up, we want to stop, we don't believe we can get past it. We
adopt an attitude of, "I tried one way to get it done and it didn't
work." So what? Try another way. Keep trying. Keep working
through it. The question is: how big is your why? Your why is why
you're doing it. If your why is big enough, you'll find a way around

the obstacle – any obstacle. Everyone is going to come up against obstacles and everyone will face difficult circumstances, it's part of life, the key is to create a big *why*.

In an earlier chapter we talked about the fact that you will have to go through trials in life. You will have to go through situations, so *expect* to have to go through them and *expect* to find a way to get around them because that's the only way you're going to find the success you want. In James, Chapter 1, verses 2 and 3, James tells the people:

> [2] *Consider it pure joy, my brothers, whenever you face trials of many kinds,*

> [3] *because you know that the testing of your faith develops perseverance.*

So strengthen your mental muscle. Every time you go through a trial, every time you get over an obstacle, it strengthens you. It gives you more to lean back on and it gives you the confidence to know that you can get through what lies before you. Earlier, I gave the example of when I was in basic training in the Air Force. When I was struggling, one of the things I would lean on was the fact that there were one million people already in the military. If one million people could get through, then so could I! I could be the next person to make it through; I could be number one million and one! I made it through and I've held on to that victory, and others, as I've gone on through life.

Obstacles are there so that you can build a history of success. As you build, you can look upon each victory to realize, and to remind yourself, what is possible. You can look back, but you don't live back there. Remember:

> **"Successful people remember their past, live in their present, and plan their future."**
> – *James Cooper*

So you don't live back there, you just take a peek. You look back to remember what you have already achieved and then you apply it to your current situation. You have to have a clear vision and focus on the vision, not the obstacle. If you raise your mind-sight and you look beyond the obstacle at the prize; at what you're trying to achieve, the obstacle will appear much smaller.

Finding a way through is always going to be easier with a positive mental attitude. Remember that your situation does not define who you are. The obstacle does not say what you are and your circumstances do not dictate who you are. Michael Dell was a student fixing PCs in his room when Dell was born. He didn't see himself as a starving student, he saw himself as someone providing a service to other people. He then saw an opportunity to expand on what he did and the rest is history. So who you are is not defined by your circumstances or your obstacles. Who you are is defined by your attitude and by what you're willing to do to achieve. Another great example is Muhammad Ali. When he was stripped of his boxing title, his passport, and his boxing licence in all 50 states, he never gave up. Muhammad Ali never stopped calling himself the champ. It became just him and a small team of close people against the whole US government, but he believed that it was possible when the whole world didn't. He believed, and we know the results. You have to believe in the impossible.

In Hebrews 11:1, it says:

> [1] *Now faith is being sure of what we hope for and certain of what we do not see.*

Successful people see clearly what they want in their mind before they see it materialize. Material things are created three times:

Once mentally – you see a vision.

Once visually – you write it down; you make it plain.

Once physically – when it is created.

Years ago when Disney World was created, people felt saddened by the fact that Walt Disney himself never got to see it as he had passed before the park opened. However, he *did* see it because he saw it in his mind for years before any of the rest of us did. That is how you must approach life. You have to realize that you're going to see what you're going to achieve long before anyone else does. An example of this is the achievement of putting a man on the moon. In 1961, President John F. Kennedy announced to congress that by the end of the decade we were going to have a man walking on the moon. Back then, attempts to launch an animal into low orbit had been unsuccessful as they had not survived, so this was a monumental task. But, he focused the people on the task and he believed in the impossible. By being a great leader, other people around him started to buy into the dream. The dream became a shared vision and the project started to move forward. Before the end of the decade, in 1969, Neil Armstrong was walking on the moon and saying those famous words: one small step for man, one giant leap for mankind.

In order to realize your success, you must first see it as a vision; you must then write it down, make it visual, and then your success becomes real.

In Isaiah 50:7, it says:

> [7] *Because the Sovereign Lord helps me, I will not be disgraced. Therefore I have set my face like flint, and I know I will not be put to shame.*

This verse tells us that we *know* it's going to happen. Michael Jordan said this:

> *"If you are trying to achieve, there will be road-blocks, I've had them; everybody has had them. But obstacles don't have to stop you. If you run into a wall, don't turn around and give up. Figure out how to climb it, go through it, or work around it."*
> *– Michael Jordan*

When my mentor, Bill Bailey, was speaking years ago, he gave the example of climbing a mountain.

He told the story of telling a friend he was climbing a mountain.

The friend said, "Oh no! You can't climb that mountain."

Why not?

He said, "It's icy up there."

So I'll put on those crimper things, those spikes on my boots and I'll climb up that way. "Well you know there's driving wind and rain?"

Well I'll wear a parka.

"Well there could be ice and snow."

Well I'll have one of those little hammers with the pointy points on and I'll crawl up the mountain on my hands and knees.

"Well you might freeze."

Well I'm wearing mittens. Understand this: One of two things is going to happen here. Either I'm going to get to the top of that mountain or I'm going to die getting up that mountain.

That's the type of tenacity you need. That's the type of fortitude and desire you must have to see your vision through. If you don't have that, you're not going to see it. Make the decision that you will see it through to success.

Call to Action: Build Your Perseverance

Obstacles are life's surprise quizzes, so start to study. Obstacles and bad circumstances are given to us to test our desires, to test our resolve, to test our commitments, to test our beliefs, and to test our patience. So step up to the test and succeed. You now know how to begin building your mental strength, so build it. When you step up to the test you're going to be ready. You can succeed.

Call to Action: Expand Your Problem Solving

Join or create a mastermind group to assist you and help you as you go through your challenges, and to provide support for others. Mastermind groups meet regularly to support each other and each other's projects. They guide each other, they provide solutions, they provide ideas and they work together to help achieve results. A group creates a synergy; a power of multiple people all focused in the same area and having the same mindset. If you're not already a part of a mastermind group, start to look for people around you who could form a group. Create a group to expand your thinking and to help solve problems for other people.

Take time to look back over your journal. Remember, your situations do not define you. Study how you overcame situations in your past. If you don't have a record in your journal, look back into your past. *Look* at your past but don't live there! Start to realize that you have already overcome these old situations; you have done it before. The difficulty is always that your mind downplays the challenges you've gone through in the past, because once you've achieved it, your mind wants to start coasting again. Take a moment to remember the challenges you have already faced. Remember how you felt as you faced them; remember how you got through them, and how you felt as you overcame them. Write everything down in your journal for future reference.

Find books and biographies of people who have been through similar circumstances, or of people who have come through tough challenges. Read about how they found the strength to persevere; learn how they overcame their challenges and how they made it through to the other side. By doing this, you will start to build your own strength; you will start to find ways through your own obstacles and circumstances and you will achieve the success that you've been destined to achieve.

AFTERWORD

Now that you are on the road to success, here are some tips to keep you moving forward:

1. **Guard your Mind:** you have just invested many hours and days into reprogramming your mind to make it the optimal birthing platform for success. Don't go back to your old habits or let people talk you out of your plans. You have a deeper understanding of the truth, don't let the majority tell you otherwise.

2. **Stay Hungry for Learning:** The learning never stops. Successful people are constantly challenging themselves to learn more, to find out a deeper truth about who they are, what they are supposed to do, and who

they are supposed to do it for. Never stop learning. There is a quote that says, "The day you stop learning, is the day you die."

3. **Never Become Comfortable:** Keep stretching and striving to do more. There is not a retirement plan for success. As long as you can dream, you have a new challenge before you. Keep looking forward to the next level as you enjoy the blessing of your current success.

4. **Do All Things in Perfect Balance:** Success doesn't happen in a silo. Success should happen across all aspects of your life. As you set your next set of goals, make sure you maintain a healthy balance of worship, work, prayer, and play in all you do.

5. **Pay it Forward:** You have been blessed with a new understanding of who you are, and what success truly is. Once you have learned a new skill, and practiced the principals, you have mastered it enough to become a teacher. The Lord will assign those you are supposed to teach. How will you know they're assigned to you? They will have challenges in their lives you have successfully overcome. Be a willing teacher to those who have to walk the same problem you overcame.

BOOKS
I RECOMMEND

These are just some of the timeless books I have read, or refer to:

1. **The Holy Bible** (Really, you thought I'd have some other book first?!!!)

2. **God's Inspirational Promises,** by Max Lucado

3. **The Purpose Driven Life,** by Rick Warren

4. **The Last Lecture,** by Randy Pausch

5. **Blink,** by Malcolm Gladwell

6. **Management Out of the Blue,** by MacArthur Burton

7. **Who Moved My Cheese,** by Spencer Johnson

8. **Quiet Strength,** by Tony Dungy

9. **The Millionaire Course,** by Marc Allen

10. **Rich Dad/Poor Dad,** by Robert Kiyosaki

11. **Why We Want You to be Rich,** by Donald Trum and Robert Kiyosaki

12. **Shaping History Through Prayer and Fasting,** by Derek Prince

13. **Working With Angels,** by Steven Brooks

14. **Chicken Soup for the Christian Soul 2,** Jack Canfield, Mark Victor Hansen

15. **Battlefield of the Mind,** by Joyce Meyer

16. **Lessons from the Pro,** by Tim Sanders

17. **Overcoming Time Poverty,** by Bill Quain

18. **The Seer,** by Jim Goll

19. **I Dare You!,** by William H. Danforth

20. **As a Man Thinketh,** by James Allen

21. **The Law of Success,** by Napoleon Hill

22. **It Only take a Minute to Change You Life,** by Willie Jolley

23. **Your Best Life Now,** by Joel Osteen

24. **Attitudes that Attract Success,** by Wayne Cordeiro

25. **Live Your Dreams,** by Les Brown

26. **Cure for the Common Life,** by Max Lucado

27. **The Seven Habits of Highly Effective People,** by Steven Covey

28. **Eat Mor Chikin,** by S.Truett Cathy

29. **The 21 Irrefutable Laws of Leadership,** by John C. Maxwell

30. **The 21 Success Secrets of Self-Made Millionaires,** by Brian Tracy

31. **The Go Giver,** by Bob Burg, John David Mann

ABOUT THE
AUTHOR

James R. Cooper is Co-Founder and Managing Director of Maxser Consulting Group, LLC and Pastor of Restoration International Christian Ministries. Originally from Long Island, NY, James lives in Maryland with his wife Regyna and their son Andrew.

James' professional journey began with the privilege of serving in the US Air Force as a Security Policeman and Military Working Dog Handler. While serving in the military, James was called to special assignments. James provided dignitary support for foreign leaders and heads of state, including President Ronald Reagan, Vice President George Bush, and Secretary of State Cyrus Vance. The highlight of James' military career was providing dignitary support for the United Nations 40th anniversary. Foreign leaders from around the world were in attendance. With his military tour ending, and a burning desire to compete in the 'real' world, James found himself in California starting over in the private sector.

Transitioning from the military back to the civilian world, tests both your commitment, adaptability and resolve. An unexpected encounter lead to a position as a security officer, and his corporate climb. God used that position as the door that has allowed James to manage multimillion dollar budget portfolios for several Fortune 500 corporations in a number of varying operational roles. While living in Charlotte, NC a new opportunity offered itself, in the IT field. With a seed planted by his father when he was a young boy, James knew there was more to learn and experience. With a change of direction and reduction in pay, he pressed into the new field and excelled to the point where he lead multimillion dollar projects as a Project/Program Manager.

With a drive instilled in him from his youth, to own his own business, James has successfully launched 2 organizations. With all of his professional success, the road he was about to travel was the greatest of his life.

Knowing there was more for him to do, James was called to lead and teach uncommon leaders. This seemed difficult to imagine, but when God ordains a thing, it is done. With much prayer, worship and fasting, Restoration International Christian Ministries was launched in 2010. All the doors that God has opened, has given James the opportunities to share his message of success, both at home and abroad, and has uniquely equipped him as he assists organizations and individuals to break through barriers to find their success.

CPSIA information can be obtained at www.ICGtesting.com
Printed in the USA
BVOW032256031012

302037BV00006B/248/P